Australian Stories for Children

For Clare and Goff — thanks for giving
me the love of stories.
And for John, who helped bring them to life. LK

For Jenny, Neil and Rupert. GR

Random House Australia Pty Ltd
20 Alfred Street, Milsons Point, NSW 2061
http://www.randomhouse.com.au

Sydney   New York   Toronto
London   Auckland   Johannesburg

First published in 2003
Text copyright © see acknowledgements for individual stories
Illustrations © Gregory Rogers 2003

National Library of Australia
Cataloguing-in-Publication Entry

30 Australian stories for children.

Includes index.
For upper primary school students.
ISBN 1 74051 910 8.

1. Children's stories, Australian. 2. Short stories,
 Australian. I. Knight, Linsay, 1952- . II. Rogers,
 Gregory, 1957- . III. Title : Thirty Australian stories
 for children.

A823.01089282

Cover and text design by Monkeyfish
Typeset in Goudy and Telegram by Midland Typesetters
Illustrations created with pen and ink, ink wash and Chinagraph pencil
Printed by Ligare Book Printer, Sydney

This project has been assisted by the Commonwealth Government through
the Australia Council, its arts funding and advisory body.

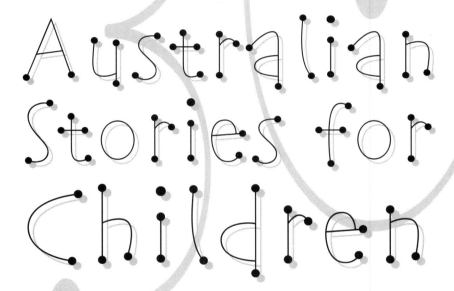

30 Australian Stories for Children

EDITED BY LINSAY KNIGHT

ILLUSTRATED BY GREGORY ROGERS

RANDOM HOUSE AUSTRALIA

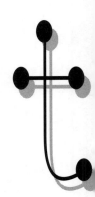

cont

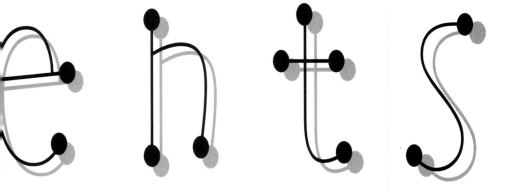

Foreword

For thousands of years Australian storytellers have captivated their audiences with tales of their ancestors, of how the world came to be, of the unusual animals and plants to be found in the Australian bush and of wild adventures experienced by people just like themselves. Some of these stories are so comical that they make us laugh out loud, others are sad and make us cry, while the scary ones make us sit on the edge of our seats, afraid to hear what happens next. But all these stories have one thing in common – they show the riches to be found in reading or listening to Australian wordsmiths describe the wide brown land they love and the antics of the imaginary characters who live there.

This collection of Australian treasures shows the depth and scope of our Australian storytelling heritage. From animal stories like *Brolga and Jabiru*, *Sing to Me* and *The Flood Maker*, first passed from one generation to another in the Aboriginal oral tradition and later collected by passionate enthusiasts, to early published stories like *Dot and the Kangaroo* and *Blinky Bill*, to later favourites like *Snugglepot and Cuddlepie*, *The Muddle-headed Wombat* and *The Silver Brumby*, all these well loved characters come alive again with each new generation of readers.

Also included are hilarious romps like *The Bugalugs Bum Thief* and *The Very Naughty Mother Goes Green* that inspire us to explore our madcap side while *My Enemy* and *Licked* have a twist in their tail and keep us guessing to the very end. And there are heroic characters like Pinquo the penguin, who saves a town from disaster, and beings from other worlds, like ghosts and angels, who interact with children in the real world and help us explore feelings and experiences we don't often talk about. All these stories help enrich our lives as they nourish our creative processes and help us understand the world around us.

Some of the stories included have never been read before – *Gran's Beaut Ute*, *Haunted*, *Moving On* and *Slam Jam Sam*, while treasured by their authors, waited for the right moment to make their entrance. And others, like *The Wish*, were specially written for this collection. Some are complete and others are part of longer stories that are worth finding and reading from the beginning to the end.

But most importantly, the stories collected here will inspire us all to seek and find our own stories – the important ones that shape and change our lives – the ones we just can't wait to write down and share with others. It's important that we learn to love stories by reading them ourselves or listening to them be read but also that we become story collectors and story tellers like the authors celebrated here. So welcome to the world of stories.

Linsay Knight

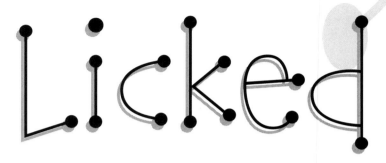

Licked

PAUL JENNINGS

1

TOMORROW when Dad calms down I'll own up. Tell him the truth. He might laugh. He might cry. He might strangle me. But I have to put him out of his misery.

I like my dad. He takes me fishing. He gives me arm wrestles in front of the fire on cold nights. He plays Scrabble instead of watching the news. He tries practical jokes on me. And he keeps his promises. Always.

But he has two faults. Bad faults. One is to do with flies. He can't stand them. If there's a fly in the room he has to kill it. He won't use fly spray because of the ozone layer so he chases them with a fly swat. He races around the house swiping and swatting like a mad thing. He won't stop until the fly is flat. Squashed. Squished – sometimes still squirming on the end of the fly swat.

He's a dead-eye shot. He hardly ever misses. When his old

fly swat was almost worn out I bought him a nice new yellow one for his birthday. It wasn't yellow for long. It soon had bits of fly smeared all over it.

It's funny the different colours that squashed flies have inside them. Mostly it is black or brown. But often there are streaks of runny red stuff and sometimes bits of blue. The wings flash like diamonds if you hold them up to the light. But mostly the wings fall off unless they are stuck to the swat with a bit of squashed innards.

2

Chasing flies is Dad's first fault. His second one is table manners. He is mad about manners.

And it is always my manners that are the matter.

'Andrew,' he says. 'Don't put your elbows on the table.'

'Don't talk with your mouth full.'

'Don't lick your fingers.'

'Don't dunk your biscuit in the coffee.'

This is the way he goes on every meal time. He has a thing about flies and a thing about manners.

Anyway, to get back to the story. One day Dad is peeling the potatoes for tea. I am looking for my fifty cents that rolled under the table about a week ago. Mum is cutting up the cabbage and talking to Dad. They do not know that I am there. It is a very important meal because Dad's boss, Mr Spinks, is coming for tea. Dad never stops going on about my manners when someone comes for tea.

'You should stop picking on Andrew at tea time,' says Mum.

'I don't,' says Dad.

'Yes you do,' says Mum. 'It's always "don't do this, don't do that". You'll give the boy a complex.'

I have never heard of a complex before but I guess that it is something awful like pimples.

'Tonight,' says Mum, 'I want you to go for the whole meal without telling Andrew off once.'

'Easy,' says Dad.

'Try hard,' says Mum. 'Promise me that you won't get cross with him.'

Dad looks at her for a long time. 'Okay,' he says. 'It's a deal. I won't say one thing about his manners. But you're not allowed to either. What's good for me is good for you.'

'Shake,' says Mum. They shake hands and laugh.

I find the fifty cents and sneak out. I take a walk down the street to spend it before tea. Dad has promised not to tell me off at tea time. I think about how I can make him crack. It should be easy. I will slurp my soup. He hates that. He will tell me off. He might even yell. I just know that he can't go for the whole meal without going crook. 'This is going to be fun,' I say to myself.

3

That night Mum sets the table with the new tablecloth. And the best knives and forks. And the plates that I am not allowed to touch. She puts out serviettes in little rings. All of this means that it is an important meal. We don't usually use serviettes.

Mr Spinks comes in his best suit. He wears gold glasses and he frowns a lot. I can tell that he doesn't like children. You can always tell when adults don't like kids. They smile at you with their lips but not with their eyes.

Anyway, we sit down to tea. I put my secret weapon on the floor under the table. I'm sure that I can make Dad crack without using it. But it is there if all else fails.

The first course is soup and bread rolls. I make loud slurping noises with the soup. No one says anything about it. I make the slurping noises longer and louder. They go on and on and on. It sounds like someone has pulled the plug out of the bath. Dad clears his throat but doesn't say anything.

I try something different. I dip my bread in the soup and make it soggy. Then I hold it high above my head and drop it down into my mouth. I catch it with a loud slopping noise. I try again with an even bigger bit. This time I miss my mouth and the bit of soupy bread hits me in the eye.

Nothing is said. Dad looks at me. Mum looks at me. Mr Spinks tries not to look at me. They are talking about how Dad might get a promotion at work. They are pretending that I am not revolting.

The next course is chicken. Dad will crack over the chicken. He'll say something. He hates me picking up the bones.

The chicken is served. 'I've got the chicken's bottom,' I say in a loud voice.

Dad glares at me but he doesn't answer. I pick up the chicken and start stuffing it into my mouth with my fingers. I grab a roast potato and break it in half. I dip my fingers into the margarine and put some on the potato. It runs all over the place.

I have never seen anyone look as mad as the way Dad looks at me. He glares. He stares. He clears his throat. But still he doesn't crack. What a man. Nothing can make him break his promise.

I snap a chicken bone in half and suck out the middle.

It is hollow and I can see right through it. I suck and slurp and swallow. Dad is going red in the face. Little veins are standing out on his nose. But still he does not crack.

The last course is baked apple and custard. I will get him with that. Mr Spinks has stopped talking about Dad's promotion. He is discussing something about discipline. About setting limits. About insisting on standards. Something like that. I put the hollow bone into the custard and use it like a straw. I suck the custard up the hollow chicken bone.

Dad clears his throat. He is very red in the face. 'Andrew,' he says.

He is going to crack. I have won.

'Yes,' I say through a mouth full of custard.

'Nothing,' he mumbles.

Dad is terrific. He is under enormous pressure but still he keeps his cool. There is only one thing left to do. I take out my secret weapon.

4

I place the yellow fly swat on the table next to my knife.

Everyone looks at it lying there on the white tablecloth. They stare and stare and stare. But nothing is said.

I pick up the fly swat and start to lick it. I lick it like an ice cream. A bit of chewy, brown goo comes off on my tongue. I swallow it quickly. Then I crunch a bit of crispy, black stuff.

Mr Spinks rushes out to the kitchen. I can hear him being sick in the kitchen sink.

Dad stands up. It is too much for him. He cracks. 'Aaaaaagh,' he screams. He charges at me with hands held out like claws.

I run for it. I run down to my room and lock the door. Dad yells and shouts. He kicks and screams. But I lie low.

Tomorrow, when he calms down, I'll own up. I'll tell him how I went down the street and bought a new fly swat for fifty cents. I'll tell him about the currants and little bits of licorice that I smeared on the fly swat.

I mean, I wouldn't really eat dead flies. Not unless it was for something important anyway.

PAUL JENNINGS was born in Heston, near London, on 30 April 1943, and was six when he came to live in Melbourne with his parents and sister. After he left school he decided to be a teacher and went to Frankston Teachers College. He taught for a while before studying at the Lincoln Institute to become a speech pathologist. Then he worked as a Lecturer in Special Education before moving to the Warrnambool Institute of Adult Education in 1979 to work as a Senior Lecturer in Language and Literature. He stayed there for ten years until he began writing full-time. *Unreal!* was published in 1985. Paul lives in a house overlooking the ocean. His books have won many awards and he was appointed Member in the General Division of the Order of Australia (AM) in the Australia Day 1995 Honours List for service to children's literature.

My Enemy

CHRISTINE HARRIS

WE'VE BECOME accustomed to living with danger, but I have an uncomfortable feeling about today's mission. My group is restless. They probably realise that I'm nervous. But we have no choice about venturing out. The weather's about to change and we haven't enough to eat. There is food nearby but it's always a risk. Often we end up carrying back not just supplies, but the bodies of our friends.

Their species and ours have been enemies for years. I don't know why it should be like this, but it is. They're a peculiar race and find us threatening. Once we were intrigued by other civilisations and longed to increase our understanding. It was our dream. But that was long ago. Now we are hard pressed just to stay alive, and want to be left alone.

It's not like me to be so depressed. Perhaps I'm getting old. My usefulness to the others will soon be over and with things as tough as they are, I know what my fate will be. Survival is everything. I shudder. Concentrate, I must concentrate. Should we stay hidden or run? It's a difficult choice.

The enemy stalks through the underbrush not bothering to hide his presence. And why should he? He's stronger and he knows it.

A young warrior at the back of the group bolts and heads for home. I can't restrain him. He's too quick. It's undisciplined but I don't blame him. We all know the enemy has a new weapon, powerful and devastating. Our losses have been great.

I consider retreating but it's too late. I see him clearly now. He's big. Everything about these creatures is like that: big bodies, big egos and now – big weapons.

There are sounds behind me and I gesture to the others to stay still. They won't do it, but I try. After all, I am the leader. The enemy looks left and right, advancing relentlessly toward us. He hesitates, uncertain of our exact position. Our size sometimes works in our favour.

I know what will happen, but I can't prevent it. Maybe it's fate. All I can do is meet my enemy with pride. He stops. He stares. His voice booms out but he speaks in a foreign language and the words are lost. But his meaning is clear. The troops scatter, panic-stricken. They have no means of protecting themselves against such a giant. Zig-zagging blindly they run over the hillside. I take one last look at the blue sky above our heads, then charge forward. Better to be mown down moving forward than backward. I race towards my enemy in a frenzy. He roars. Then I feel it. The very thing I most dreaded.

It drifts down from above and coats my body, strangely cool at first, then white hot. There is no defence against chemical warfare. My legs cramp. I can run no further. My body begins to quiver. I shake so badly that I wonder whether I will actually break into pieces. But at least this way I might not be devoured by my family.

Unsure that he has finished the job off properly, the enemy reaches down, his massive hand blocking out the light. I'm helpless as he aims the can directly at my feeble body and squirts more poison right at me. The pain is unbearable and I am racked with spasms. Against a cold-blooded enemy like this human, we ants have no hope.

CHRISTINE HARRIS writes anywhere – at her desk or in Pizza Huts, in motels and on planes, on the beach and in bed. She loves eating chocolate and brie cheese, discovering new flowers in her cottage garden and telling stories. Christine has written more than 30 books, including short stories, science fiction, historical novels, picture books and poetry. Her work has been published in Australia and internationally.

Brolga and Jabiru

RETOLD BY
ROLAND ROBINSON

IN THE DREAMTIME, two tribesmen, Janaran, the jabiru, and Bonorong, the brolga, met at a billabong.

'What are you going to do?' asked Janaran.

'I'm going to look out for lily-roots, and I want to be able to fly,' said Bonorong.

'Well,' said Janaran, 'I'm going to look out for fish, and I want to be able to fly, too.'

'But how are we going to do this?' asked Bonorong.

'Why,' said Janaran, 'we'll have to make ourselves feathers. I'm going to have white feathers with green and black bands down my wings. I'll have a dark blue neck and head, and I'll have red-yellow legs.'

When he said this, he began to dance. He held out his arms like outspread wings and cried out, 'Klock, klock, klock, kerluk.' He ran along the ground with his arms beating like wings and began to fly up through the trees.

Janaran circled the tops of some high paperbark trees and then came gliding down to rest in front of Bonorong. He closed his wings. 'Klock, klock,' he said, strutting about. 'Do you see my feathers, and how I can fly?'

'Yes, yes,' cried Bonorong. 'I'm going to make feathers now. I'll be blue-grey, with a grey breast. I'll have red on the sides of my head, and I'll have yellow legs.' Then Bonorong held out his arms like outspread wings and began to dance.

'Arr-arr-arr, preek-preek-eek-eek-preek,' he sang out. He too ran along the ground with his arms outspread like wings and flew away high over the trees and the wide plain beyond. Then he circled and came gliding in to rest and fold his wings in front of Janaran.

'Now I've got feathers!' cried Bonorong as he stood on his toes and stretched his neck and flapped his wings. 'Now that I can fly,' he cried, 'I'm going over the plains to find a dry billabong where there are lily-roots.'

'Yes, that's right,' said Janaran. 'You have to look out for lily-roots, and I have to look out for fish.'

Then Bonorong opened his wings and flew off through the trees. 'Bo-bo' (Good-bye), he called as he flew away.

'Bo-bo, cumwun' (Good-bye, friend), called back Janaran.

Then Janaran stepped down into the shallows of the billabong and started wading and looking out for fish. And as he waded he sang this song to himself:

'Kadji-ooruk kalinee, kadji-ooruk kalinee, kadji-ooruk kalinee, ar-kanar, woorukee, kadji-ooruk woorukee. Kut!'

This song means, 'I see fish darting this way, and fish darting that way. Here's one I can spear. Kut!' This is the sound his bill makes in the water as he spears a fish.

This is the song of Janaran, one of the songs that are sung to the bamboo drone-pipe in the Djauan tribe.

ROLAND ROBINSON was born at Belbriggan, near Dublin, in 1912 but from the age of nine he has lived in Australia. When he was fourteen he was working on a sheep station, and later became a boundary rider, and then a jockey at country race-meetings. For many years Roland collected stories from tribal Aborigines all over Australia and in 1946 began to write down the tales he had been told. He received a Commonwealth Literary Fellowship and several grants so that he could continue to collect and publish Aboriginal stories.

Dot Meets a Deadly Snake

EXCERPT FROM *DOT AND THE KANGAROO*
ETHEL PEDLEY

WHEN DOT AWOKE, she did so with a start of fear. Something in her sleep had seemed to tell her that she was in danger. At a first glance she saw that the Kangaroo had left her, and coiled upon her body was a young black Snake. Before Dot could move, she heard a voice from a tree, outside the cave, say, very softly, 'Don't be afraid! Keep quite still, and you will not get hurt. Presently I'll kill that Snake. If I tried to do so now it might bite you; so let it sleep on.'

She looked up in the direction of the tree, and saw a big Kookaburra perched on a bough, with all the creamy feathers of its breast fluffed out, and its crest very high. The Kookaburra is one of the jolliest birds in the bush, and is always cracking jokes and laughing, but this one was keeping as quiet as he could. Still he could not be quite serious, and a smile played all round his huge beak. Dot could see that he was nearly bursting with suppressed laughter. He kept on saying under his breath,

'What a joke this is! What a capital joke! How they'll all laugh when I tell them.' Just as if it was the funniest thing in the world to have a Snake coiled up on one's body; when the horrid thing might bite one with its poisonous fangs, at any moment!

Dot said she didn't see any joke, and it was no laughing matter.

'To be sure *you* don't see the joke,' said the jovial bird. 'Onlookers always see the jokes, and I'm an onlooker. It's not to be expected of you, because you're not an onlooker'; and he shook with suppressed laughter again.

'Where is my dear Kangaroo?' asked Dot.

'She has gone to get you some berries for breakfast,' said the Kookaburra, 'and she asked me to look after you, and that's why I'm here. That Snake got on you whilst I flew away to consult my doctor, the White Owl, about the terrible indigestion I have. He's very difficult to catch awake; for he's out all night and sleepy all day. He says cockchafers have caused it. The horny wingcases and legs are most indigestible, he assures me. I didn't fancy them much when I ate them last night, so I took his advice and coughed them up, and I'm no longer feeling depressed. Take my advice, and don't eat cockchafers, little Human.'

Dot did not really hear all this, nor heed the excellent advice of the Kookaburra not to eat those hard green beetles that had disagreed with it, for a little shivering movement had gone through the Snake, and presently all the scales of its shining black back and rosy underpart began to move. Dot felt quite sick as she saw the reptile begin to uncoil itself, as it lay upon her. She hardly dared to breathe, but lay as still as if she were dead, so as not to frighten or anger the horrid creature, which presently seemed to slip like a slimy cord over her bare legs, and wriggled away to the entrance of the cave.

With a quick, delighted movement, she sat up, eager to see where the deadly Snake would go. It was very drowsy, having slept heavily on Dot's warm little body; so it went slowly towards the bush, to get some frogs or birds for breakfast. But as it wriggled into the warm morning sunlight outside, Dot saw a sight that made her clap her hands together with anxiety for the life of the jolly Kookaburra.

No sooner did the black Snake get outside the cave, than she saw the Kookaburra fall like a stone from its branch, right on top of the Snake. For a second, Dot thought the bird must have tumbled down dead, it was such a sudden fall; but a moment later she saw it flutter on the ground, in battle with the poisonous reptile, whilst the Snake wriggled and coiled its body into hoops and rings. The Kookaburra's strong wings, beating the air just above the writhing snake, made a great noise, and the serpent hissed in its fierce hatred and anger. Then Dot saw that the Kookaburra's big beak had a firm hold of the Snake by the back of the neck, and that it was trying to fly upwards with its enemy. In vain the dreadful creature tried to bite the gallant bird; in vain it hissed and stuck out its wicked little spiky tongue; in vain it tried to coil itself round the bird's body; the Kookaburra was too strong and too clever to lose its hold, or to let the Snake get power over it.

At last Dot saw that the Snake was getting weaker and weaker for, little by little, the Kookaburra was able to rise higher with it, until it reached the high bough. All the time the Snake was held in the bird's beak, writhing and coiling in agony; for he knew that the Kookaburra had won the battle. But, when the noble bird had reached its perch, it did a strange thing; for it dropped the Snake right down to the ground. Then it flew down again, and brought the reptile back to the bough, and dropped it once more – and this it did many times. Each time the Snake moved less and less, for its back was being broken by these falls. At last the Kookaburra flew up with its victim for the last time, and, holding it on the branch with its foot, beat the serpent's head with its great strong beak. Dot could hear the blows fall – whack, whack, whack – as the beak smote the Snake's head; first on one side, then on the other, until it lay limp and dead across the bough.

'Ah, ah, ah! Ah, ah, ha!' laughed the Kookaburra, and said to Dot, 'Did you see all that? Wasn't it a joke? What a capital joke! Ha, ha, ha, ha, ha! Oh, oh, oh! How my sides do ache! What a joke! How they'll laugh when I tell them.' Then came a great flight of kookaburras, for they had heard the laughter, and all wanted to know what the joke was. Proudly the Kookaburra told them all about the Snake sleeping on Dot, and the great fight. All the time, first one kookaburra, and then another, chuckled over the story, and when it came to an end every bird dropped its wings, cocked up its tail, and throwing back its head, opened its great beak, and all laughed uproariously together. Dot was nearly deafened by the noise; for some chuckled, some cackled; some said, 'Ha, ha, ha!' others said, 'Oh, oh, oh!' and as soon as one left off, another began, until it seemed as though they couldn't stop. They all said it was a splendid joke, and that they really must go and tell it to the whole bush. So they flew away, and far and near, for hours, the bush echoed with chuckling and cackling, and wild bursts of laughter, as the kookaburras told that grand joke everywhere.

ETHEL PEDLEY was born in 1860 in London. Ethel played the violin and made her living as a music teacher. Her story of *Dot and the Kangaroo* can be enjoyed by readers of all ages and makes a plea for conservation of the bush and its animals. In the preface Ethel wrote: 'To the children of Australia in the hope of enlisting their sympathies for the many beautiful, amiable, and frolicsome creatures of their fair land, whose extinction, through ruthless destruction, is being surely accomplished.' Ethel died in 1898, at the age of 38.

Bett-Bett

EXCERPT FROM *THE LITTLE BLACK PRINCESS*
MRS AENEAS GUNN

BETT-BETT must have been a princess, for she was a king's niece; and, if that does not make a princess of anyone, it ought to do so.

She didn't sit – like fairy-book princesses – waving golden sceptres over devoted subjects, for she was just a little bush blackfellow-girl, about eight years old. She had, however, a very wonderful palace – the great, lonely, Australian bush.

She had, also, one devoted subject – a little, speckled dog called Sue; one big trouble – 'looking out tucker'; and one big fear – debbil-debbils.

It wasn't all fun being a black princess, for nobody knew what terrible things might happen any minute – as you will see.

Once, when Bett-Bett and Sue were camped with some of the tribe on the Roper River, they were suddenly attacked by the Willeroo blacks, who were their very fiercest enemies. Everybody 'ran bush' at once to hide, with the Willeroos full chase after them. In the fright and hurry-scurry, Bett-Bett fell into the river, and at once decided to stay there, for, in spite of the crocodiles, it was the safest place she could think of. She swam under the water to the steep banks, and caught hold of the roots of an old tree. Standing on this, she stuck her nose and mouth out of the water, in the shelter of a water-lily leaf; and, there she stood for a long time without moving a muscle, her little naked black body looking exactly like one of the shadows.

When all was quiet and it was getting dark, she crept out, thinking she would be safe for the night. Sue at once came out from her hiding-place, and, licking Bett-Bett's hand, seemed to say, 'My word, that *was* a narrow escape, wasn't it?'

Bett-Bett spoke softly to her, and the two of them then hunted about to see if any tucker had been left behind.

Sue very soon found a piece of raw beef; and Bett-Bett made a fire in the scrub, so that nobody could see the smoke. Then, while the supper was cooking, they crouched close to the warmth, for they felt very cold.

By and by, the steak caught fire, and Bett-Bett picked it up between two sticks, and tried to blow it out. Finding she could not manage this, she laid it on the ground, and threw a handful of earth on it; and, at once, the flames died away.

She and Sue then grinned at each other as if to say, 'Aren't we clever? We know how to manage things, don't we?' and were just settling down to enjoy their supper, when somebody grabbed Bett-Bett from behind, and shouted out, 'Hallo! What name you?'

Did you ever see a terribly frightened little black princess? I did, for I saw one then. The Maluka and I were out-bush, camping near the river. We had arrived just about sunset, and, seeing black tracks, had decided to follow them, and found Bett-Bett. Big Mac, one of the stockmen, was with us, and it was he who had caught hold of her; but, if it had been an army of debbil-debbils, she could not have been more frightened.

'Nang ah! Piccaninny,' I said, meaning 'Come here, little one'. I spoke as kindly as I could, and Bett-Bett saw at once that I was a friend.

She spoke to Sue and came, saying, 'Me plenty savey Engliss, Missus!'

This surprised us all, for she looked such a wild little girl. I asked her where she had learnt her 'plenty savey Engliss'; and she answered, 'Longa you boys', meaning she had picked it up from our homestead boys.

After a little coaxing, she told us the story of the Willeroos, and said 'Dank you please, Missus', very earnestly when I asked if she would like to sleep in our camp.

As we went up the bank, I was amused to see that she was munching her beef. It takes more than a good fright to make a blackfellow let go his only chance of supper. After a big meal of damper and honey – 'sugar-bag' she called it – she went to a puddle, and smeared herself all over with mud; and, when I asked why she did this, she said, 'Spose skeeto come on, him bite mud, him no more bite meself'; and I thought her a very wise little person.

As soon as it became dark, she and Sue curled themselves up into a little heap near the fire, and fell asleep for the night.

In the morning, I gave her a blue and white singlet that I had taken from one of the boys' swags. She dressed herself in it at once, and looked just like a gaily coloured beetle, with thin black arms and legs; but she thought herself very stylish, and danced about everywhere with Sue at her heels. Sue was the ugliest dog of any I had seen. She looked very much like a flattened out plum pudding on legs, with ears like a young calf, and a cat's tail.

As we sat at breakfast, I asked Bett-Bett if any mosquitoes had bitten her in the night. 'No more,' she said, and then added with a grin, 'Big mob bin sing out, sing out'. She seemed pleased to think how angry they must have been when they found a mouthful of mud, instead of the juicy flesh they expected.

When we were ready to start for the homestead, I asked Bett-Bett if she and Sue would like to come and live with me there. 'Dank you please, Missus!' she answered, grinning with delight.

So Bett-Bett found a Missus, and I – well, I found a real nuisance.

JEANNIE GUNN was born Jeannie Taylor in Melbourne, in 1870. After leaving the University of Melbourne, she and her sister opened a private school in Hawthorn. In 1901 she married Aeneas Gunn and they moved to Elsey cattle station at Warloch Ponds on the Roper River, south-east of Katherine, in the Northern Territory. Jeannie's husband died in 1903 and she returned to Melbourne. She wrote *Little Black Princess* in 1905 and *We of the Never-Never* in 1908, which was made into a film in 1982. Jeannie was awarded an OBE in 1939 and died in 1961.

I Want to See a Human

EXCERPT FROM *SNUGGLEPOT AND CUDDLEPIE*
MAY GIBBS

HERE ARE the adventures of Snugglepot and Cuddlepie. They were foster-brothers, and this is how it came about.

When Cuddlepie was very small – that is, when he had only been out of the bud a few hours – a great wind arose and, lifting him out of his mother's arms, carried him far across the tops of many trees and left him in a spider-web.

This saved his life, but again he nearly lost it, for a short-sighted old bird, mistaking him for a grub, was about to eat him up, when a Nut, beholding, shouted, 'Bird! Bird! Mind the snake.'

The old bird, very frightened, flew away. Then the kind Nut climbed up the spider-web, lifted up the little cold, weeping baby and gently carried him home.

Now this was the home of Snugglepot, and that kind Nut was his father.

Here then lived Cuddlepie, side by side with Snugglepot, and they grew strong and fat . . .

One day a wise old Kookaburra came to the neighbourhood. All the Blossoms and Nuts crowded in to hear him speak.

He said, 'I am old! I have travelled! I have seen Humans! Humans are strong as the Wind, swift as the River, fierce as the Sun. They can scratch one stick upon another and, lo, there will be a Bush Fire. They love the Fire. The male Human carries it about in his skin and the smoke comes out of his nostrils. They whistle like the birds; they are cruel as the snake. They have many skins which they take off many times. When all the skins are off the Human looks like a pale frog.'

Now Snugglepot and Cuddlepie were scared all over to hear of these things, so they went often to listen to the wise Kookaburra.

'These Humans,' said Mr Kookaburra, 'are as bad as bad, but there must be bad things in this world as well as good. It would be very awkward for me if there were no snakes to eat.'

And Snugglepot and Cuddlepie thought very much about it all.

One day they asked Mr Blue-cap Wren if it were all true. 'Quite,' said he, 'I have some relations living in the Sydney Domain, and I know.'

'I want to see a Human,' said Snugglepot.

'In the distance,' said Cuddlepie.

One very hot night, when the Cicadas were singing so loudly that Snugglepot couldn't hear his father snoring he and Cuddlepie crept out of bed and out of the house.

'Where are you going?' asked Cuddlepie.

'To see the Humans,' said Snugglepot.

'Only in the distance,' pleaded Cuddlepie. Then they began their journey.

◆

[One day, Snugglepot went with their friend little Ragged Blossom] to buy clothes and he forgot all about poor Cuddlepie.

So Cuddlepie waited and waited and waited, till he grew tired and fell asleep again.

While he was asleep he had a dream. He thought someone was calling him, so he got up and followed the voice; and he really did get up and walk along, though he was fast asleep all the time.

'Cuddlepie, come here!' the voice kept calling, and as it called, Cuddlepie followed, with eyes wide open, yet fast asleep, till by and by he came to a little stream. When his foot touched the water, he woke up.

'Help me, help me,' called a faint voice near him.

'Where are you?' called Cuddlepie.

'I'm here. Help me,' came the voice more faintly.

Cuddlepie scrambled, and pushed, and tore his way through the sticks, and leaves, and ferns till he came to an open space at the foot of a big tree. Then he stood in horror. He saw a terrible thing. A great iron trap was there, chained to a stake, and tightly shut were its great iron teeth — shut upon the arm of a poor grey Possum. Tears were running down his face, and the big, gentle brown eyes looked at Cuddlepie in an agony of pain.

'Oh! Poor dear Possum! Who did this to you?' asked Cuddlepie.

'Humans,' said the Possum. 'They set these traps at our very doors and we run into them before we see them.'

Cuddlepie was too unhappy to speak. He went to the stream and brought back some water in his cap, but the Possum was quite still and his eyes were shut.

'Oh!' said Cuddlepie in anguish, 'Possum, dear Possum, don't say you're dead!' But the Possum lay quite still.

◆

Suddenly Snugglepot remembered Cuddlepie. He thought he heard his voice calling in the distance.

It was Cuddlepie.

When he had seen the poor Possum lying so still, he had grown frightened, and shouted, 'Help! Help!! Help!!!' And he shouted louder and louder, till Snugglepot heard him and coo-eed back and came hurrying to find him, while little Ragged Blossom, who was hiding, crept out and came after him. A lot of Bush creatures were running in the same direction, and quite a crowd had gathered by the time Snugglepot reached the place.

When Cuddlepie saw Snugglepot he burst into tears, and cried, 'See! Oh, see what the Humans have done.'

Snugglepot was filled with grief and the tears ran down his cheeks, while all the Bush creatures cried in their own way. Nothing could be done. No one was strong enough to open the great trap. The poor, gentle Possum must stay there till he died.

Now, as everyone stood there weeping for pity, a great noise came sounding on the breeze. All the Bush creatures turned pale. 'Humans! Humans!' they cried, and scuttled away, tumbling over each other in their haste to hide.

Snugglepot and Cuddlepie stood spellbound as the great noise came nearer. Then little Ragged Blossom ran to Snugglepot. 'Come, hide quickly!' she cried, and led them up the Possum track to a cave in the side of the tree.

Just as they reached it a monster Dog came crashing through the Bush and stood over the trap barking, while close behind him came a monster Human.

'Why, it looks like a giant nut,' said Snugglepot, 'and he's got eyes like ours.'

'Look! What's he doing?' whispered Cuddlepie. 'Oh! Oh! He's going to kill the poor Possum.'

But no! The monster Human opened the trap with his strong hands and gently lifted out the little Possum. Then he bound up the poor broken leg, and they heard him say, 'These rotten traps, I hate them.' And he pulled up the stake and flung the trap into the stream. Then he said, 'Come on,' to the monster Dog, and they both walked away through the Bush.

Snugglepot and Cuddlepie and little Blossom were amazed. When all sounds of the monsters had died away, they hurried down to the Possum. His eyes were open, and he gladly drank some water. Soon he was so much better that they helped him home.

'Well,' said Snugglepot, when they were at last on the road again by themselves. (Ragged Blossom had stayed to help Mr Possum.) 'Well!' he said. 'We have seen a Human.'

'Yes,' said Cuddlepie.

'And a kind one, too,' said Snugglepot.

'I wish,' said Cuddlepie, 'that all Humans were kind to Bush creatures like that.'

MAY GIBBS, artist and author, was born on 17 January 1877 in Surrey, England and arrived in Western Australia with her parents when she was two. She later studied art in England. *The Gumnut Babies*, her first book about Australian bush fairies, was published in 1916 in Sydney. Apart from her famous *Snugglepot and Cuddlepie* (1918), her books include *Flower Babies*, *Wattleblossom Babies*, and other Gumnut fairytale books. May had a deep love and understanding of the Australian bush, which she aimed to pass on to children through her books. She was appointed MBE for her services to Australian literature. May died on 27 November 1969.

The Flood-Maker

A TRADITIONAL STORY RETOLD BY
JEAN CHAPMAN

ONCE there was a huge frog, the hugest frog ever known. He was called Tiddalik.

Tiddalik woke one morning with a thirst which was greater than his size. He started to drink. He drank the water in the creeks, in the swamps, in the billabongs and the lakes, in the ponds and pools and rivers. He drank until there was no fresh water left in his part of the world.

Everywhere, creatures began to die because there was no water to drink. Trees dropped their leaves because they had no moisture. The grass turned brown. Earth became dust. Very soon, Tiddalik would be the only creature left alive.

The animals could not think of a way to find water, until they listened to Platypus, an old and wise fellow. 'Make Tiddalik laugh,' he said. 'Once he laughs the water he has drunk will come pouring out of his mouth.'

So everyone hurried and scurried to the giant frog's resting place. And for a long time they tried to make Tiddalik laugh. Kookaburra told his funniest stories. He told them so well he started laughing himself before he had finished.

But Tiddalik did not laugh.

Kangaroo jumped over Emu.

Still Tiddalik didn't laugh.

Scaly Lizard waddled up and down, up and down, on his short legs. He made his stomach poke out.

It was no use. Tiddalik didn't laugh.

The animals were in despair. What could they do? What *could* they do? Then, from his dry creek bed, Nabunum, the Eel, slithered towards the giant frog.

Nabunum began to dance. He started with slow graceful movements. Then his dance grew faster and faster. He wriggled, twisted, wriggled, twisted and turned into strange shapes. And as he danced his long tail flicked and tickled, flicked and tickled, flicked and tickled the frog's huge round stomach. Suddenly, Tiddalik's eyes lit up. His great round stomach shook. The whole of Tiddalik's enormous body began to shake. He began to laugh. He threw back his head and laughed, and water gushed from his mouth to stream away over the country. It flowed into the creeks, the swamps, the billabongs and the lakes, the ponds and pools and rivers.

There was water again for everyone. And Tiddalik, the great frog, disappeared. He was never seen again in that part of the country.

Sing to Me

A TRADITIONAL STORY RETOLD BY
JEAN CHAPMAN

ONCE a baby Turtle was asleep under a bush. His mother and father had left him there in the shade while they explored the beach. It was a hot morning. Soon the sun was right overhead. Mother Turtle crawled back to the sea. Father Turtle crawled back to the sea. Each thought Baby Turtle was with the other. But he was still asleep in the shade of the bush.

When he woke, oh dear, he was hot! He began to cry.

He cried for his mother and father. They didn't hear him.

Wild Dog did. He came bounding up to the baby Turtle and nosed him about. 'That's a lovely song you're singing! Will you sing it all over again from the beginning?'

'I'm not singing! I'm crying,' sniffled Little Turtle.

'That's *never* crying!' said Wild Dog. 'You were singing, and such a song to delight my old ears. I want to hear more of it. Come on, now. Sing up!'

'You are mistaken, sir,' said Little Turtle. 'Turtles don't sing. I truly can't sing one note.'

'You are only saying that to annoy me,' Wild Dog barked. 'If you don't sing, then . . . then I'll eat you up.'

The baby Turtle was so shocked he stopped crying altogether. He said in a stout brave voice, 'All right! Eat me up! Do what you like! Bake me in the sun! Stew me in a pot! Grill me on a fire! Sizzle me in a pan! Do all of those things, but please, *please*, whatever you do, don't throw me in the sea.'

'Why not?' asked Wild Dog.

'I don't want to drown.'

'Oho! So you're afraid of water!' snarled Wild Dog, winking his mean little eyes. 'Oho! You're afraid of the sea! All right, I won't throw you in if you sing me a song, just a little song.'

'But I can't sing,' said Little Turtle. 'So I won't sing.'

'Then into the sea you go,' snapped Wild Dog. 'Headfirst into the deep cold sea!'

'Please, please! Don't throw me into the sea,' screamed Little Turtle.

'Too late! Too late!' howled Wild Dog. He swaggered to the water's edge with Little Turtle in his mouth. He swung Little Turtle to and fro, then let him go.

Baby Turtle sailed through the air and over the waves, to smack down in the water, far out from the beach. Down he went, then up he came. His head bobbed above the water. 'Thank you!' he laughed. 'It feels good to be back home again!' Then Little Turtle ducked under the deep, cool water, leaving Wild Dog on the beach, stamping his feet and howling because he had missed out on a turtle lunch.

JEAN CHAPMAN was born in Sydney in the late 1920s. She is one of Australia's most famous re-teller of traditional tales for children. In the 1950s she began writing stories for preschool children for the ABC *Kindergarten of the Air* radio program and went on to write for television. She is best-known for her themed collections of stories, poems and songs, such as *Velvet Paws and Whiskers* (on cats) and *Pancakes and Painted Eggs* (on Easter).

Introducing The Bomb

EXCERPT FROM *DON'T PAT THE WOMBAT!*
ELIZABETH HONEY

THE BOMB

INTRODUCING MR BRIAN CROMWELL otherwise known as Crom the Bomb, or simply The Bomb.

He was sent to our school from another school where I bet they had a massive 'The Bomb's Gone Off!!!' party when he left.

None of the parents like him, and at the end of the year the Principal had a queue of parents who announced loudly, 'Whatever happens I do not want my child in Mr Cromwell's class next year.'

Mr Cromwell became a teacher so he could be bossy and mean. He should have gone into the army. Occasionally he is OK. I heard he was nice for a day back in 1876.

I was in his class last year. He has a funny walk and he's a sneaky bottle-basher, a grog artist. He thinks nobody knows he drinks, but everybody does.

They put Cromwell teaching the grade fours. They wouldn't dare give him the tender little preps. It would be cruelty to dumb animals. Besides, prep mothers are like mother bears and they would tear him down with their claws and rip him to shreds. If he had grade six it would be open warfare, and kids would bring bazookas to school, so they buried him in the middle with poor old grade four. A couple of kids left our school rather than be in The Bomb's class.

The parents were furious.

'Why don't they sack him?' said Jude from next door.

Mum was mending my jeans. 'You can't just sack a teacher. It's a great rigmarole: letters of complaint, days to respond, support groups, counselling, the whole catastrophe. Besides, we can't prove he's done anything wrong.'

'Why does he keep teaching?'

'Well frankly,' said Mum with a sigh, trying to undo a knot in the cotton, 'I think he enjoys it.'

This year my brother lost the lottery. He got put in The Bomb's class. Even he didn't deserve that. At least he was with his best mate, Max.

'I'm sorry Adrian,' said Mum. 'Let's just see how we go. It's only for a year.'

ONLY for a YEAR! What does she think that is? Two days? A year is forever!

Mum went on. 'Remember how you didn't want to be in Mrs McDonald's, and it turned out fine? Well, you never know, this year might turn out fine, too.'

'Yeah,' I added. 'The Bomb might get struck by lightning. Be thankful, Adrian,' I said with brotherly concern. 'Just be glad he's not your dentist.'

You know something, all the teachers, the Principal, 'The whole school community', the School Council and a tribe of angry parents couldn't shift The Bomb . . . but Jonah did.

HOW TO BE UNPOPULAR IN FIVE EASY LESSONS THE BRIAN CROMWELL WAY

1 GO OFF LIKE A BOMB

You think you're doing the right thing then suddenly he goes psycho at you. *Detention!*

2 BE MEAN

Once, on a school outing, after twenty minutes on the bus, Phillip, this little kid, says, 'I want to go to the toilet.' Well, The Bomb didn't remind us about going before we got on the bus. Us big kids could hang on, but this little kid sat hunched up with his skinny legs crossed and twisted round, looking miserable and pathetic. We all knew how he felt.

Faith Williamson and Kristelle went up and said, 'Mr Cromwell, Phillip really badly wants to go to the toilet.'

Cromwell told them to mind their own business. Would he stop the bus? NO WAY!!!!!

Phillip wasn't making any noise, but he had tears in his eyes, and his legs were red where they pressed together so hard. And we drove on and on and on and on for kilometres and the whole bus was whispering. In the end you can guess what happened. I bet that was the worst day in Phillip's life.

3 BE SLACK

In the whole of last year he set two projects. We had to have them in exactly on time. A couple of kids were late. *Detention!*

But he didn't look at those projects for ages and ages.

'When are we getting our projects back, Mr Cromwell?' asks Faith Williamson.

'Never!' whispers someone up the back. *Detention!*

So unfair. Kids in other classes got hologram stickers saying 'Fabulous', 'Far out', 'Neat', and their teachers wrote nice stuff about what they'd done. But we'd get our projects back about two months later with one word, like 'Fair'. We didn't even try to do good work. What was the point?

4 DO SLOW TALK

The Bomb loves to hear his own voice. When he gets mad he talks slowly, letting the words drip out one by one.

'I suppose you think it doesn't matter if the toilets look like a swamp' and he rocks backwards and forwards on his heels. Then he hurls the thunderbolt. *Detention!*

Once, after a magnificent performance of slow talk, when he took about an hour to say thirty words, the whole class plotted together and we wrote our homework

all

spaced   out

like   this   .

Guess what happened. Starts with the letter D. But he got the message because he didn't do any slow talk for a couple of weeks after that. (Beth the Good did her homework properly and she got detention, too! Probably for being such a goodie goodie!)

D × 28 = us

5 GIVE DETENTIONS

Besides the D-word, The Bomb has an arsenal of mean tricks up his sleeve. If you rock back on your chair, he makes you kneel at your desk, and that hurts so badly.

If you leave a crumb after eating lunch, you have to clean up the whole school ground.

If you're not paying attention, he does his ruler trick, eg: Matos is asleep up the back; The Bomb creeps up beside him, takes Matos's ruler and smashes it down on the table, right by his ear; Matos leaps out of his skin; the ruler is toothpicks.

On the first day of school I said to Adrian, 'I dare you to ask The Bomb the meaning of tyre ant.' My brother got the first detention of the year. For impertinence. Look it up.

And it was all quadruply unfair because I had the best teacher in the southern hemisphere, the gorgeous Miss Cappelli . . .

ELIZABETH HONEY was born on 7 February 1947 in Wonthaggi, in Victoria. She grew up on a dairy farm with her two sisters and one brother. After finishing school Elizabeth went to art college, travelled overseas and then became an illustrator. First she drew pictures for other people's books and then she started writing and illustrating her own stories. She has won many awards and her books are published throughout the world. Elizabeth lives in Melbourne with her family and likes bushwalking, cycling, reading, singing and films.

The Bugalugs Bum Thief

TIM WINTON

SKEETA ANDERSON woke up one summer morning to find that his bum was gone.

He lay back on his bed and tried not to get upset. I'm still asleep, he thought. I'm dreaming! But he could hear the crows cawing in the tree outside his window – blaah, blaah, blaah! And he heard boat engines starting up down at the jetty, too, so he knew he was awake.

He was *not* happy.

Skeeta Anderson knew that his bum was gone because, as any sensible person knows, a missing bum makes a large dent in the back of a person. You feel like a turtle without a shell, a donkey without a tail.

There were other clues, too. When Skeeta sat on the edge of his bed, he slid straight to the floor. Nothing to sit on! Walking from his bedroom to the kitchen he lost his pyjama pants – there was nothing to hold them up!

'Mum!' he called. 'Dad! Something terrible –'

He stopped and stared. His mum and dad were eating breakfast on the floor.

'Morning Skeet,' said his mum.

Skeeta's mouth dropped open like a truck door.

'Ahem,' said Skeeta's dad, sounding very embarrassed. 'We seem to have lost our bottoms in the night. Finding it hard to sit on our chairs. Useful thing, a bottom, when you think of it.'

Skeeta's parents went on eating their toast and drinking their tea.

'Don't be late for school,' said Skeeta's mum.

Skeeta lived in a small town by the sea. The town was called Bugalugs. No one could remember who was to blame for thinking up such a dumb name for a town, and even if they could remember, no one was going to own up to it. Because the people of Bugalugs were a bit proud. They were nice folks, but just a teeny bit vain.

Bugalugs was three streets wide and was built next to a beautiful bay where fishing boats anchored. Behind the town was a great desert of white dunes.

Every morning, before the sun came up over the dunes, the fishermen of Bugalugs went out to catch crayfish. They put fresh bait in their traps every day and the little red critters made gutses of themselves. As all sensible people know, a cray will eat anything except football boots, so bait is not hard to find. Every day crayfish were pulled from the traps, still munching, and were sent all over the world so people could munch on *them*. That's how it was every day at Bugalugs.

Except today.

Skeeta went to the window and saw Billy Marbles trying to ride past on his bike. Billy was sliding all over the place, with his knees hanging over the handlebars, and there was Billy's sister Mavis walking to school with a big dent in the back of her dress.

Skeeta ran out into the street, holding up his PJ's, and right away he saw it. The whole town was the same. No bums!

He ran inside and got dressed quickly. With some string he tied his trousers on.

Then he ran to his best mate's house.

Mick Misery, his best mate, was always getting a hiding. Mick's mum was a real smacker. Smacking was her hobby. She walloped Mick for being early, she whacked him for being late. But this morning she wasn't getting anywhere at all. When Skeeta arrived, Mick's mum was swinging away but every hit just swished past because Mick Misery was *bumless.*

Mrs Misery gave up glumly and sent them off to school. Mick whistled like a drunk canary but Skeeta was worried.

Maybe it's the ozone layer, he thought. Or perhaps we're under attack from aliens. But there had to be an easier answer.

It was an awful day at school. With nothing to sit on or hold their pants up with, the kids at Bugalugs Primary didn't get time to learn much. At lunch, Billy Marbles couldn't play doogs at all. As any sensible person knows, a bum gives you balance and you can't be school marble champ without balance. The footy team was useless, the netballers got depressed.

During spelling, Mr Wally's shorts suddenly sprang off their safety pins and went scurrying down his long hairy legs like rats out of a tree. The kids laughed. They cacked themselves. *And* they all went home with piles of homework so big they needed their dads' wheelbarrows to get it all home.

After school, instead of doing his homework, Skeeta Anderson decided to do some detective work. He wrote it all out on a piece of paper. No one was talking about it all, embarrassed as they were, but it was pretty clear to Skeeta that:

- at least 169 bums are missing
- scientific instruments show no alien interference
- binoculars show no missing bots plugging up the hole in the ozone layer.

So, he figured: someone must have them. Someone must have burgled them, sneaked into everyone's bedroom with a torch and a pair of salad tongs and got away with the lot!

But Skeeta was a clever kid, a bit of a scientist, really. Because, as any sensible person knows, you can't hide a townful of bums very easily. And in a town where barely anyone has a pair of buttocks to their name, any person about still wearing one was definitely SUSPICIOUS.

So Skeeta wired on a pair of running shorts and began to investigate.

At the Bakery, Hairy Hans was sweeping up, looking sad.

'No one wants buns today, Skeet,' said Hans. 'Not that I can blame them. No doughnuts either.'

Nothing suspicious here.

Skeeta went on to Mr Rood the butcher who had a RUMP STEAK SPECIAL sign in his greasy window. That seemed a bit dodgy, today of all days, so Skeeta sneaked a look in the coolroom while the butcher was serving a customer. Nothing. Besides, Mr Rood had been burgled same as everyone else.

Nothing at the general store or the petrol station, and Mrs Huge from the pub looked like a meat pie with a bite taken out of it.

He tried the tip. There was always something useful at the tip, and the price was always right, but no second-hand backsides here today.

In the dunes he saw Mick Misery sliding down slopes having a great time. Skeeta kept out of sight. Mick was the only kid in town enjoying not having something in the back of his shorts and Skeeta didn't want to spoil his fun.

Through the streets of Bugalugs, Skeeta Anderson ran. Dogs snapped at him but missed by a margin. There was nothing suspicious at all, though the number of bums missing must be about four hundred or more by now, he figured.

Down at the beach, windsurfers complained that their wetsuits were turning into sails, and girls in bikinis had to wear suspenders. The seagulls laughed cruelly. Skeeta looked at them hard and long, but they didn't look fat enough to be the culprits. Fishermen stood around looking miserable. They'd all been seasick today and had come in early. As any good fisherman will tell you, bums equals balance. But someone on the jetty caught Skeeta's eye.

A fisherman, big and gruff-looking, with tattoos on his arms and a belly under his singlet like a beer barrel, walked right past, and Skeeta's hair stood on end. A-HA! Follow that bum!

Skeeta followed him all the way up the beach and down a sand track which led to a big shed with a truck parked out the front. There was the smell of oil and stinky fish and rotten crays, but also a strange pink smell he couldn't quite name.

The man slid the shed door open and went in. All the big, black greasy blowflies that had been sticking to the door suddenly pounced on Skeeta who was trying to hide behind the truck.

Slowly, Skeeta crept forward until he reached the door and put his eye to a crack. What a sight! He turned and ran like fury.

Constable Coma was asleep as usual when Skeeta came busting into the police station, but he woke quickly.

'Strike me pink!' said the constable. 'Someone's stolen me –'
'Everyone's!' said Skeeta. 'Follow me!'

They pounded off to the shed, though not very quickly

because Constable Coma kept losing his pants and handcuffs and just about everything else on the way. People noticed them. It wasn't often they saw the policeman running away anywhere so they followed. Soon the whole town was on their trail.

It was getting dark when they got to the shed – Skeeta, Constable Coma, and the whole population of Bugalugs. There was a light on inside. Skeeta pulled the door open and everyone roared.

There it was, a gigantic stockpile of human bums, bottoms, backsides and buttocks reaching almost to the roof. Four hundred and ninety-six units, all still in good condition (though some in better shape than others).

The fisherman sat down, looking ashamed.

'Why do you need four hundred and ninety-six citizens' bottoms, for goodness sake?' asked Constable Coma.

'For bait,' said Skeeta Anderson.

The crowd growled. Constable Coma put the handcuffs on Blue Murphy and lost his pants yet again.

'Righto, everyone can come inside and claim their own property.'

But the people of Bugalugs hummed and hahed, and shuffled their feet. They got all embarrassed.

'Someone turn the lights out,' said Skeeta.

And when the lights were out everyone went mad. It was like a footy match in there. Hairy Hans liked the feel of a smooth pink one at the bottom of the pile. Skeeta's mum (who had a torch) saw one right up high that was small and peachy and when she climbed up, the pile began to quiver and shake.

Billy Marbles snatched one for himself and his sister Mavis took *two*. And then all those bottoms came crashing down on the crowd, clunking and bonking like ten tonnes of over-ripe watermelons, shaking the ground, buckling the walls of the shed, sending the blowflies out to sea in a panic, and when someone finally turned the lights on the town nearly died laughing.

After that night Bugalugs got back to normal. Well, almost normal. People looked a bit strange. Because they'd all been too proud to take their own bottoms back, fat people had skinny ones and bald people had hairy ones. People pretended to be happy with their new choices, but really they were miserable. It was uncomfortable, unhygienic and altogether unsavoury, like wearing someone else's false teeth.

So the next Saturday Skeeta organised a swap-meet in the town hall and everyone got their own bum back.

All except Skeeta's best mate Mick Misery. Mick did a special deal. He bought Blue Murphy's for twenty-eighty cents and three black marbles.

It was too big for him by far, but it was as hard as a brick and his mum gave up smacking him overnight.

Everyone was grateful to Skeeta Anderson. They bought him rump steaks, buns and doughnuts and they always thought of him as the kid who caught the Bugalugs Bum Thief.

TIM WINTON was born in 1960 in Western Australia. His first novel, *An Open Swimmer*, won the Vogel Award in 1981, and since then Tim has never looked back, being one of the few Australian authors to write full-time. His books for children include *Jesse* (1988), *Lockie Leonard, Human Torpedo* (1990), *The Bugalugs Bum Thief* (1991), *Lockie Leonard, Scumbuster* (1993), *Lockie Leonard, Legend* (1997) and *The Deep* (1998). In recent years he has become the patron of the Tim Winton Award for Young Writers, which is sponsored by the City of Subiaco in Western Australia. Tim lives in Western Australia with his wife and three children.

I Wasn't Good at Anything

STAND-UP COMEDY ROUTINE BY GARRY GAGGS
EXCERPT FROM *SELBY'S SELECTION*
DUNCAN BALL

I WASN'T GOOD at anything. I was a hopeless student. I just couldn't be bothered to study. So my parents sent me to ballet school. They thought that would keep me on my toes.

I read a book about a witch. For a while I actually wanted to be a witch. But I knew it was hopeless – I couldn't *spell*.

One time I just had to pass a maths exam so I wrote all the answers on my sleeve. But I still failed: I put on my history shirt that day by mistake.

I wasn't good at anything. I really wasn't.

We had this geography lesson. The teacher asked a girl to point to where America was on a map.

Then the teacher said to me, 'Okay, now you tell me who discovered America.' I pointed to the girl and said, 'She did.'

They let me act in the school play. The play took place

in a bakery. For once I got the best *role*.

I read a book called *All about Glue*. I couldn't put it down. It's true! All of this is true!

My parents sent me to spy school. The teacher was passing out bottles of invisible ink and I said, 'Could you make mine blue?'

But seriously, folks, I couldn't stand the place. One morning I just pulled the blanket over my head and refused to get out of bed.

'What kind of an agent do you think you're going to be?' my teacher asked.

I said, 'What do you think? An undercover agent.'

I had a lesson on the electric guitar. My teacher just sat there and listened. When I finished he said, 'You ought to be on television.' I said, 'Thank you. Am I really that good?' And he said, 'No, but then I could turn you off.'

He said, 'Maybe you should be playing an easy guitar.' I said, 'An easy guitar? What's that?' And he said, 'No strings attached.'

He thought it was funny. Then he said, 'Why don't you get a rubber guitar?'

I said, 'A rubber guitar?'

And he said, 'Yes, then you could play in a rubber band!'

'That would keep you out of *treble*,' he said.

And that was my teacher! I said, 'Tell me honestly: do you think I'll ever be any good at playing this thing?' He said, 'Let's put it this way: my cats are more mewsical.' Get it? *Mews-ical*.

I mean, how was that supposed to make me feel? I wasn't good at anything.

Honest, I wasn't.

I said to my parents, 'I want to be a boxer.' And they said, 'You're too small to be a boxer. Why don't you be a cocker spaniel instead?'

And that was my parents! I couldn't win.

I went to take swimming lessons but there was no water in the pool. I said, 'How can I learn to swim when there's no water?' And the instructor said, 'Just dive in and do the crawl.'

My parents let me get a dog, but he kept biting people. They told me that I'd have to train him not to bite. I didn't know how. He never did anything I told him to. Anyway, one day they caught me feeding him garlic. 'What do you think you're doing?' my mother said. I said, 'I just wanted to be sure his bark was worse than his bite.'

My first real job was as an elevator operator. It wasn't a bad job – it had its ups and downs.

Later I worked in a shoe shop. A woman came in and said, 'I'd like some crocodile shoes.' So I said, 'How big is your crocodile?'

I thought it was a reasonable question. Anyway, we didn't have crocodile shoes so she asked for snakeskin shoes. We didn't have any of those either. So she said, 'This is hopeless! Don't you have any shoes made out of reptile skin?' I said, 'No, but we do have open-toad sandals.' Open-*toad*, get it?

I worked as a waiter. I only lasted a day. I was very slow. One of the customers got impatient and yelled at me. She said, 'Bring me a slice of cake and step on it!' I only did what she told me.

But seriously, folks, I worked as a store detective in a clothing store. There was a woman shoplifter. I chased her out of the shop and down the street but she gave me the slip. The next day the same thing happened and again she gave me the slip. The third day she gave me the dress.

I won't tell you about when I worked at a dairy milking cows. It was an *udder* disaster too.

I wasn't good at *anything!* So that's when I decided to be a comedian.

Thanks for listening. You're beautiful.

DUNCAN BALL was born in the United States and then moved around a lot with his family before coming to live in Sydney in 1974. He began work as an industrial chemist but he soon decided he wanted to fulfil his original dream of being a writer and began writing for both adults and children. Duncan is best known as the creator of the *Selby the Talking Dog* series, beginning with *Selby's Secret*. His other books include the *Emily Eyefinger* series, the *Ghost and the Gory Story* series and a number of books in the *Case Of* series. Duncan lives in Glebe with his wife and their cat, Jasper.

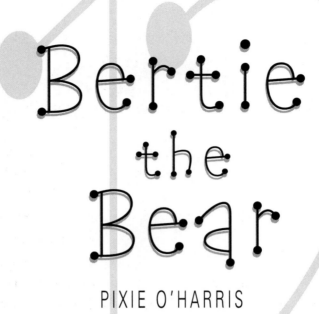

Bertie
the
Bear

PIXIE O'HARRIS

BERTIE THE BEAR loved adventure. When he was quite small, he had run away to sea. Now he was home again, and was staying with his grandmother in Gum-Tree Glade.

Bertie had made friends with Napoleon Bandicoot, Leopold Wombat, and Algernon Bilby, and called them Nappy, Leo, and Algy for short. He told them wonderful stories of his travels to other lands, stories of pirates and buried treasure on South Sea Islands, until their eyes opened larger and larger in surprise. Of course they all three wanted to run away to sea.

'Foolish creatures,' said Grannie Bear in a huff.

Bertie always talked in seaman talk, too, which Nappy, Leo and Algy tried to copy. Much to Grannie Bear's disgust, every night he insisted on climbing one of the highest gum-trees in the glade, and slinging a hammock amongst its branches. There the wind would sway his bed and make him feel that he was once more on the waves in a wild storm. Nappy, Leo and

Algy did likewise, and their mothers could not get them to sleep in hollow trunks, safe and sound from stormy weather. Moreover, the little rascals would eat nothing but sea-pie, and their mothers naturally grew tired of making it day after day.

One night Grannie Bear scolded Bertie. He looked and seemed quite ashamed of himself, and Grannie Bear felt secretly pleased as she went to bed. The next morning when she woke up and called Bertie out of her window, there was no answer. He usually cried, 'Heave-ho, my heartie, I'll be showing a leg!' as he climbed out of his hammock. But when she looked, there was no one there. Poor Grannie! She sat down and cried, thinking she had driven Bertie away with her cross words the night before.

Then there came a knock on her door. It was Mrs Bandicoot. She was weeping into a large handkerchief.

'What's the matter?' asked Grannie Bear.

'It's my sweet little Nappy. He's run away to sea with Bertie the Bear,' whimpered Mrs Bandicoot. 'See, he left me this note. You can read what it says.'

Grannie Bear put on her glasses and read:

'Dear Mother,
i am running away to see. i am not happy any more at
home.
Your loving son,
Nappy.'

'Oh, dearie me!' groaned Grannie Bear as another knock came to the door. It was Mrs Bilby. She was looking very flurried, and stuttered when she spoke.

'I've co . . . co . . . come about my Algy. He's go . . . go . . . gone across the ocean with your gran . . . gran . . . grandson. He left me this note. I'll let you read it.'

Once more Grannie put on her glasses and read:

'Dear Mum,
By the time you read this I shall be away on the water.
Maybe I'll become a pirate and kill other pirates for
treasure. Anyway I'll be all right because I'll be with
Bertie the Bear. Look after yourself.
Your son,
Algy.'

'Oh dearie, dearie me!' groaned Grannie Bear, as another
knock came to her door. In strode Mrs Wombat. She was a
large creature, with a very determined face.

'Where's that grandson of yours?' she shouted. 'Enticing my
son to run away to sea, my son who has the finest home in the
bush! Just you glance at this stupid note! As if he doesn't get
enough to eat at home.'

Wearily Grannie Bear put on her glasses and read:

'Ship ahoy, Mum,
I've been a land-lubber too long. I must away to where
the palm trees sway, where I'll have sea-pie every day,
and lots more to eat and drink. Farewell. Though we be
parted by ocean thy sailor lad will ever dream of thee.
Leo.'

'Oh, dear, dearie, dearie me!' groaned Grannie Bear.

'Just wait until I see Bertie the Bear and that sailor lad of
mine,' cried Mrs Wombat. 'I'll give him oceans and sea-pie. I'll
get a gum-switch, and go to the port and find the ship he is on,
and switch him right back here, the young rascal.'

'Yes, just you wait until I catch that young Nappy,' said Mrs

Bandicoot. 'I'll make him sorry he ever slept in a hammock and made friends with Bertie the Bear.'

'I'll come with you,' cried Mrs Bilby. 'I'll spank that s . . . s . . . son of mine until he c . . . can't sit down. Running away to sea, indeed! Wait until I can give Bertie the Be . . . Be . . . Bear a piece of my tongue.'

Just then there was another knock upon the door, and in pranced Marmaduke the Possum.

'Come with me,' he said, smiling as they followed him out of the house into the bush. He led them, still grumbling, to the edge of the billabong. Suddenly they stopped their chatter and looked in the direction in which Marmaduke was pointing.

'Ship ahoy, there!' shouted Marmaduke, making a trumpet of his paws.

The mothers stared in astonishment. Out in the middle of the lake was a large raft. The wind was making little waves on the surface of the billabong and rocking it. On the raft were four green-looking little animals. Bertie the Bear was the greenest, and he was holding on to the mast. Algy, Nappy and Leo were hanging over the sides, looking as if their last hour had come.

'And ship rhymes with dip, and boat rhymes with float,' unhappy little Nappy was wailing, while the others just moaned aloud.

'That's as far as they got,' said Marmaduke.

'My poor, darling, little Algy!' called Mrs Bilby.

'My sweet Nappy!' cried Mrs Bandicoot, beginning to sniffle.

'My precious Leo!' shouted Mrs Wombat, in a giant's voice. 'Come back to Mother. Come back.'

'My beautiful Bertie! Just wait until I get you home!' muttered Grannie Bear under her breath.

PIXIE O'HARRIS, illustrator and author, was born Rhona Olive Harris on 15 October 1903, in Cardiff, in Wales. In 1920 her family migrated to Australia and settled in Perth before moving to Sydney the following year. It was while on the ship to Australia that she adopted her new first name after hearing people refer to her as 'the Welsh pixie'. A change in her surname followed when her first work was published, after a printer at the *Sydney Morning Herald* added an apostrophe to her second initial. During Pixie's career she contributed poems, stories and illustrations to many publications, as well as illustrating the work of other authors. Her own books include *The Pixie O'Harris Story Book* (1940) and *Marmaduke the Possum* (1942). In 1939, at the time of the birth of her third daughter, she found the hospitals cold and clinical and decided to paint fairy-style murals for children. Over 50 children's hospital wards, schools, day nurseries and baby clinics throughout New South Wales have been decorated with her work. Pixie O'Harris died on 17 April 1991 in Sydney.

Bunyip Bluegum Leaves Home

EXCERPT FROM *THE MAGIC PUDDING*
NORMAN LINDSAY

UNFORTUNATELY, in the hurry of leaving home, [Bunyip Bluegum] had forgotten to provide himself with food, and at lunch time found himself attacked by the pangs of hunger.

'Dear me,' he said, 'I feel quite faint. I had no idea that one's stomach was so important. I have everything I require, except food; but without food everything is rather less than nothing.

'I've got a stick to walk with.
I've got a mind to think with.
I've got a voice to talk with.
I've got an eye to wink with.
I've lots of teeth to eat with,
A brand new hat to bow with,
A pair of fists to beat with,
A rage to have a row with.
No joy it brings

To have indeed
A lot of things
One does not need.
Observe my doleful plight.
For here am I without a crumb
To satisfy a raging tum –
O what an oversight!'

As he was indulging in these melancholy reflections he came round a bend in the road, and discovered two people in the very act of having lunch. These people were none other than Bill Barnacle, the sailor, and his friend, Sam Sawnoff, the penguin bold.

Bill was a small man with a large hat, a beard half as large as his hat, and feet half as large as his beard. Sam Sawnoff's feet were sitting down and his body was standing up, because his feet were so short and his body so long that he had to do both together. They had a pudding in a basin, and the smell that arose from it was so delightful that Bunyip Bluegum was quite unable to pass on.

'Pardon me,' he said, raising his hat, 'but am I right in supposing that this is a steak-and-kidney pudding?'

'At present it is,' said Bill Barnacle.

'It smells delightful,' said Bunyip Bluegum.

'It is delightful,' said Bill, eating a large mouthful.

Bunyip Bluegum was too much of a gentleman to invite himself to lunch, but he said carelessly, 'Am I right in supposing that there are onions in this pudding?'

Before Bill could reply, a thick, angry voice came out of the pudding, saying –

'Onions, bunions, corns and crabs,
Whiskers, wheels and hansom cabs,

Beef and bottles, beer and bones,
Give him a feed and end his groans.'

'Albert, Albert,' said Bill to the Puddin', 'where's your manners?'

'Where's yours?' said the Puddin' rudely, 'guzzling away there, and never so much as offering this stranger a slice.'

'There you are,' said Bill. 'There's nothing this Puddin' enjoys more than offering slices of himself to strangers.'

'How very polite of him,' said Bunyip, but the Puddin' replied loudly –

'Politeness be sugared, politeness be hanged,
Politeness be jumbled and tumbled and banged.
It's simply a matter of putting on pace,
Politeness has nothing to do with the case.'

'Always anxious to be eaten,' said Bill, 'that's this Puddin's mania. Well, to oblige him, I ask you to join us at lunch.'

'Delighted, I'm sure,' said Bunyip, seating himself. 'There's nothing I enjoy more than a good go-in at steak-and-kidney pudding in the open air.'

'Well said,' remarked Sam Sawnoff, patting him on the back. 'Hearty eaters are always welcome.'

'You'll enjoy this Puddin',' said Bill, handing him a large slice. 'This is a very rare Puddin'.'

'It's a cut-an'-come-again Puddin',' said Sam.

'It's a Christmas steak and apple-dumpling Puddin',' said Bill. 'It's a – . Shall I tell him?' Sam asked, looking at Bill. Bill nodded, and the Penguin leaned across to Bunyip Bluegum and said in a low voice, 'It's a Magic Puddin'.'

'No whispering,' shouted the Puddin' angrily. 'Speak up. Don't strain a Puddin's ears at the meal table.'

'No harm intended, Albert,' said Sam, 'I was merely remarking how well the crops are looking. Call him Albert when addressing him,' he added to Bunyip Bluegum. 'It soothes him.'

'I am delighted to make your acquaintance, Albert,' said Bunyip.

'No soft soap from total strangers,' said the Puddin', rudely.

'Don't take no notice of him, mate,' said Bill. 'That's only his rough and ready way. What this Puddin' requires is politeness and constant eatin'.'

They had a delightful meal, eating as much as possible, for whenever they stopped eating the Puddin' sang out –

'Eat away, chew away, munch and bolt and guzzle,
Never leave the table till you're full up to the muzzle.'

But at length they had to stop, in spite of these encouraging remarks, and, as they refused to eat any more, the Puddin' got out of his basin, remarking – 'If you won't eat any more here's giving you a run for the sake of exercise,' and he set off so swiftly on a pair of extremely thin legs that Bill had to run like an antelope to catch him up.

'My word,' said Bill, when the Puddin' was brought back. 'You have to be as smart as paint to keep this Puddin' in order. He's that artful, lawyers couldn't manage him. Put your hat on, Albert, like a little gentleman,' he added, placing the basin on his head. He took the Puddin's hand, Sam took the other, and they all set off along the road. A peculiar thing about the Puddin' was that, though they had all had a great many slices off him, there was no sign of the place whence the slices had been cut.

'That's where the Magic comes in,' explained Bill. 'The more you eats the more you gets. Cut-an'-come-again is his name, an' cut, an' come again, is his nature. Me an' Sam has been eatin' away at this Puddin' for years, and there's not a mark on him. Perhaps,' he added, 'you would like to hear how we came to own this remarkable Puddin'.'

'Nothing would please me more,' said Bunyip Bluegum.

NORMAN LINDSAY was born on 22 February 1879 in Ballarat, in Victoria. He was one of ten children – six boys and four girls. A childhood illness forced him to stay indoors so he used the time to teach himself how to draw. In 1895, Norman went to live with his brother Lionel in Melbourne, where he worked as a freelance illustrator. In 1901, the brothers joined the staff of the Sydney *Bulletin*, a weekly newspaper, magazine and review. There they drew caricatures, cartoons and illustrations on demand. Norman moved to Springwood, in the Blue Mountains, in 1912 to develop his writing talents. He wrote and illustrated *The Magic Pudding* in 1918. Norman died on 21 November 1969.

The Wish

DEBORAH ABELA

I'VE NEVER been very brave, ask anyone and they'll tell you, but the night the angel fell through the roof of my tree house, something changed in me forever.

The crash was so loud it should have woken the whole neighbourhood, but when I looked out my bedroom window, everything seemed normal except for a strange glow coming from my tree house. I turned to go back to bed and heard a pained cry. I wondered what to do. Then I heard another and knew I had no choice.

I crept into the backyard and climbed the ladder, which was a series of planks Dad and I had nailed to our tree. The wind was running amok through the leaves, flinging branches across the doorway and making it hard to see inside, but as I got closer, the light glowed brighter. Then I saw him, lying on top of two crumpled wings, a great gaping hole in the roof. He slowly sat up and rubbed his head.

'Look what you've done,' he complained.

I looked around. 'Me?'

'Yes you. If your stupid tree house wasn't in the way I would have made a perfect landing.'

He tried to move his wings but they wouldn't work. A look of worry dripped down his face. He took an hour glass from his pocket and watched the falling sands.

'There's no time,' he breathed, then said with irritation, 'and since this is your fault, you'll have to do it.'

I couldn't answer. I just stood staring.

'Here's the address.' He handed me a piece of paper. 'It's my first job so it'll be easy. They never give you hard ones to start with. Deliver this and get back as soon as you can.'

'Who . . . what . . . ?'

He sighed, annoyed at having to explain. 'My name is Linus. I'm an angel. This is my first job and if you don't deliver this within twenty minutes, I'll be the laughing stock of trainee angels everywhere.'

'You're a trainee . . . angel?'

'Everyone's got to start somewhere and as fascinating as your questions are, they'll have to wait.' He took a ball of light from his pocket. 'Take this.'

'I'm not allowed to accept things from strangers,' I said more as an excuse.

Linus looked at me like he was wondering of all the tree houses he could have fallen through, why did he have to pick mine. 'If you don't do it, I'll stay here forever and make your life a misery.'

I tried not to look afraid. 'How?'

He fixed me with a non-angelic eye. 'I know you like Flavia Bertroni and every time you try to talk to her I'll make your lips inflate like two sausages.'

I was being blackmailed by an angel but I've never been much of a fighter, so I took the ball of light and put it in my pyjama pocket.

Linus looked pleased with himself. 'Leave the wish in Graham's basket and your work will be done.'

The look on my face told him I had no idea what he meant.

'The ball of light is the wish,' he spelt out. 'And Graham is the cat at that address.'

I looked down at the piece of paper.

'Old Lady Dobbs! I'll never make it out of there alive.'

His eyes shifted before he did something else. He started crying.

'But she's a poor defenceless old lady and I'm an *almost* angel trying to help the world by doing a good deed.'

He cried even louder. It was getting embarrassing.

'Okay, okay,' I gave in.

'Excellent.' His tears dried up and I thought I saw his wings straighten, before falling back into their rumpled state. 'See you back here in fifteen minutes.'

Old Lady Dobbs lived at the end of my street. Most kids would walk the three extra blocks to school rather than go near her house. We were convinced she put curses on people, and when Billy Franks poked out his tongue at her and came down with tongue rash, we knew we were right. Mum said that was ridiculous and made me walk straight past her, enduring a new taunt every day. Old Lady Dobbs had lived there for about a hundred years with a ginger cat that mysteriously appeared the day her husband died. The cat, I now knew, was called Graham.

I felt weird as I crept along the side of her house. Not only because I was trespassing but if Mum and Dad knew I was out this late, my life would be porridge. I peeked in the lounge room window. Old Lady Dobbs was asleep on a chair, probably dreaming of new ways to terrorise the neighbourhood and Graham was lying on her lap, scraggy and sick-looking.

I slowly opened the window and climbed inside. The TV hissed a mangled static sound and blanketed the room in a pulsing blue. It was creepy. Graham was having trouble breathing and there was a dried salty tear on the old woman's face. What was I doing here? Was Flavia really worth it? She didn't even know I existed and having fat lips might at least make me more noticeable.

Then, Old Lady Dobbs cried out. A terrible shrieking cry. My nerves bunched up. My life, every boring minute of it, flashed before me and the wish flew out of my hands, into the air and straight into Graham's basket. Just as I thought I was done for, Old Lady Dobbs stopped yelling and went back to sleep.

I didn't need any more hints to get out of there. I ran home, into the backyard and scrambled up the ladder of the tree house but when I looked inside, Linus was gone and the roof was fixed like he'd never been there.

I turned and sat down in the doorway, looking over the neighbourhood. I felt pretty good. I'd never done anything dangerous before but I had no one to tell and even if I did, no one would have believed me.

The next day I tensed up as I walked past Old Lady Dobbs' house. She was sitting on the verandah as Graham scooted around her feet, chewing on his small, glowing ball. She didn't seem to notice me, so I slowed down and stopped. She could have looked up at any moment but I didn't care. I even wanted her to. I started walking again, pulling my bag across my shoulders, knowing today was the day I'd say hello to Flavia.

DEBORAH ABELA completed a Communications Degree majoring in Writing and Film Studies before entering the world of children's television. She spent six years at Cheez TV (Network Ten), writing, editing and directing for 6 to 16 year olds. Deb's experience in children's television has taught her that comedy keeps the kids watching, and she uses that to great effect in her highly successful *Max Remy Superspy* series.

Haunted

VICTOR KELLEHER

HERE IS WHAT Susie did at bedtime every night. She tiptoed into her darkened room, ran quickly across the carpet, and jumped into bed. She never dared look under the bed. She didn't let so much as a toe stick out over the edge. Her big sister had told her what would happen if she did. Something might reach up from below and grab her. Something might tug her out of bed and pull her down and down into the . . .

But it was too scary to imagine. She had heard stories about the ghosts and monsters that hid under beds, and she never wanted to meet one. She didn't even want to think about them. With a shiver, she clenched her eyes shut and went straight to sleep.

◆

In that very same room, here is what Giffin did every night. He tiptoed from a darkened corner, hurried across the carpet, and dived *under* the bed. He never dared peek out. He didn't let so much as the tip of his nose show. His big brother had told him what would happen if he did. Something might reach down and grab him. Something might tug him out from under the bed and pull him up and up into . . .

But it was too scary to imagine. He had heard stories about horrible humans who slept on the top of beds. He certainly never wanted to meet one. He didn't even want to think about them. With a shudder, he opened his eyes wider than ever and didn't sleep a wink.

◆

Things stayed that way for months and months. Then early one morning, just before dawn, everything changed. As the clock in the passage struck five, Susie's eyes flicked open. She was suddenly wide awake.

At exactly the same moment, Giffin's eyes clicked shut. He was suddenly fast asleep.

So there they were. Susie on top of the bed, staring into the dark. Giffin underneath it, sleeping peacefully down amongst the dust and balls of fluff.

He was snoring too!

It was his snoring that frightened Susie. Every time he breathed in, it was like the howling of hungry wolves. Every time he breathed out, it was like the clanking of rusty chains. She'd never been so scared in all her life. She tried hiding under the blankets, but the creepy noises floated up through the mattress. She tried blocking her ears, but his snores still made the bed tremble.

She was trembling by then. She couldn't even get her voice to work properly. 'H-e-l-p!' she croaked, and made a dash for the door. But her feet tangled in the sheet, and she fell with a crash.

◆

The noise woke Giffin. He could hear someone crying and moaning. Every time she sobbed, it was like a stab of burning sunshine. Every time she moaned, it was like an icy wash of morning light. He'd never been so scared in all his afterlife. He tried huddling in amongst the fluff-balls, but the terrible noises floated down through the mattress. He tried blocking his ears, but her sobs still made the floor tremble.

He was trembling too by then. He couldn't even get his voice to work properly. 'H-e-l-p!' he jibbered, and made a dash for the darkest corner. But his feet slipped on the fluff-balls, and he fell with a splat.

◆

That was when Susie saw it: a ghostly white blob with wide staring eyes. It was gazing at her through the dark.

That was when Giffin also saw it: a solid pinkish blob. It was gazing back at him.

'Wh-wh-who are y-y-you?' asked Susie in a terrified whisper.

'Wh-wh-who are *y-y-you*?' asked Giffin in a hollow voice.

'M-m-my name is S-s-susie. I'm a p-p-person.'

'M-m-my name is G-g-giffin. I'm a g-g-ghost.'

Once they'd admitted the awful truth, it didn't seem so awful any more. Susie even noticed that Giffin's soft white body was rather nice to look at. It reminded her of silvery moonlight. And Giffin noticed that Susie's soft brown hair was rather beautiful. It reminded him of shadows stirred gently by the night wind.

'What are you doing in my room?' Giffin wondered aloud.

'What are you doing in *my* room?' Susie corrected him.

In his creakiest voice, he explained how he had always lived in this same room in this same house with the same ghostly family. When he had finished, Susie explained how she and her family lived there as well.

Giffin was shocked. 'You mean our house is haunted by humans?'

'And ours by ghosts?' Susie added.

◆

Round about then, dawn started to break. As the first grey light stole into the room, Susie noticed something peculiar happening. Giffin's eyes were growing dimmer by the moment; and the round blob of his body began fading away.

'Giffin!' she said, surprised. 'Where are you going?'

'Susie!' he called back, as she also began to fade. 'Where are *you* going?'

Frantically, they reached for each other. They had forgotten about being afraid of creatures that might grab them in the dark. All they wanted now was to keep each other there.

But Susie's hand swept only empty space. And Giffin's brushed nothing more solid than shadows.

'Come back!' Susie pleaded, as sunlight peeped through a gap in the curtains.

'Come back!' she heard Giffin reply, his voice fainter than the creak of a distant door.

◆

With a sigh, Susie lay down amongst the tangled bedclothes. She was lying there still, fast asleep, when her mum came to wake her later that morning.

'My goodness!' she exclaimed. 'What a racket you were making in the night. Anyone would think you'd seen a ghost.'

At the very same instant, up in the gloomy old attic, a far spookier voice was saying, 'My badness! What a noise you made last night. Anyone would think you'd seen a human.'

Susie and Giffin smiled a secret smile.

'Maybe I did,' they answered together.

VICTOR KELLEHER was born in London on 19 July 1939 and came to Australia in 1976 after living in South Africa and New Zealand. Victor's books have won and been shortlisted for many awards, including the Children's Book Council of Australia Book of the Year Award. His books include, *Master of the Grove* (1982), *Taronga* (1986), *Beyond the Dusk* (2000) and *Goblin in the Bush* (2002). He now writes both children's and adult's novels full-time from his home in Bellingen, New South Wales.

Born in the Wild Wind

EXCERPT FROM *THE SILVER BRUMBY*
ELYNE MITCHELL

ONCE there was a dark, stormy night in spring, when, deep down in their holes, the wombats knew not to come out, when the possums stayed quiet in their hollow limbs, when the great black flying phalangers that live in the mountain forests never stirred. On this night, Bel Bel, the cream brumby mare, gave birth to a colt foal, pale like herself, or paler, in that wild, black storm.

Bel Bel had chosen the birthplace of the foal wisely. He was on springy snowgrass under a great overhang of granite that sheltered them from the driving rain. There he lay, only a pale bundle in the black dark, while Bel Bel licked him clean and nuzzled him. The wind roared and howled through the granite tors above in the Ramshead Range, where the snow still lay, but there was no single sound of animal or bird except the mournful howl of a dingo – once, twice, it rang out and its echo answered, weird and wild.

Bel Bel lifted her head at the sound, and her nostrils dilated. From the shadowy mass between her forefeet came a faint nickering cry and she nuzzled him again. She was very alone with her newborn foal, and far from her own herd, but that was how she had felt it must be. Perhaps because of her colour, so much more difficult to hide than bay, or brown, black, or grey or chestnut, she had always led a hunted life, and when a foal was going to be born she was very nervous and hid herself far away. Of the three foals she had had, this was the only one creamy, like herself.

Bel Bel felt a surge of pride, but the pride was followed by fear. Her son would be hunted as she was and as her own cream mother had been before her – hunted by man, since they were so strange-looking in the wild herds. And this colt would have another enemy too, every stallion would be doubly against him because of his colour.

The wind roared and the rain was cold, so cold, as if it would turn to snow. Even with the shelter of the rock, the storm was beating down on them, the moving darkness was becoming a thing of terror. The howl of the dingo came again. Bel Bel nosed the tiny colt to get up.

He heaved up his head, stuck his long forelegs out in front of him, and gave a little snort of fear. Bel Bel pushed him up till he stood, his feet far apart, long legs trembling; then she nosed him, wobbling, bending, step by step to the sandy mouth of a cave, and there, just out of the rain, she let him tumble down again.

Soon it would be time to make him drink, but for the moment, out of the wild storm, he could rest. Dawn must come soon, and in this storm there would be no men abroad to see a cream brumby mare lead her newborn foal through the snowgums to where there would be grass for her to eat and longed-for water to drink. Bel Bel really knew that there would be very few men in the mountains till all the snow had gone and they came driving their herds of red-and-white cattle, but the fear of Man was never far from her thoughts.

Dawn came very slowly, showing first the dark outline of the cave mouth against a faintly lighter sky, then, on the hill-side below them, reaching long fingers of forest right up to the rocks, the wind-tormented heads of snowgums, driven and lashing as though they must tear themselves up by the roots. The rain had stopped.

Great massing clouds kept racing up over the mountains, but, as the light grew strong, the sky began to look as if *it* was being torn in shreds by the wind. Flying streamers of rain-washed blue sky appeared and Bel Bel, feeling very hungry herself, decided it was time the foal should drink and that the day would be fair enough for a newborn colt to go with his mother to some better pastures.

'I will call you Thowra,' she said, waking him with her nose, 'because that means wind. In wind were you born, and fleet as the wind must you be if you will live.'

On that first day, while the storm blew itself out, Bel Bel did not take Thowra far, only down through the snowgums to a long glade that led to a heather-banked creek where she could drink. That night they went back to the opening of the cave and the foal slept on the dry sand curled up against his mother's flank.

The next day she decided to take him farther, to a wide, open field in the snowgum forest, where the grass grew very sweetly, even as early in the spring as this, and where the creek ran shallow over a sand and mica bottom.

The storm had died in the night and there was warm spring sunshine. Bel Bel noticed with pride how the foal trotted more strongly by her side. She did not hurry him, often stopping to graze as they moved under the snowgums or in the long glades. She never left the shelter of the trees without first pausing and looking carefully into the open country ahead. Thus it was through a curtain of the leathery snowgum leaves that she looked out on to the wide, sunny field, and saw a bay brumby grazing in the distance by the creek.

Bel Bel became completely still, watching: then she recognized the bay as a mare of her own herd, Mirri, who had been caught by a stockman as a yearling, and managed to get free. Mirri, for this reason, was very nervous of men, and she and Bel Bel had often run together, away from the herd, when they thought the others were too close to the stockmen's huts.

Now Bel Bel made out a dark shape on the ground near Mirri and knew that the bay mare, too, had her foal. Unafraid, she led Thowra out to join them.

When Mirri saw them coming she gave a whinny of greeting, and Bel Bel arched her neck a little and stepped proudly beside her creamy son, thinking how his mane and tail were silver and would someday look like spray from a waterfall as he galloped.

Mirri was pleased to see her.

'Well met, Bel Bel,' she said, 'and what a fine foal you have – creamy too! I must stir my sleepy-head to show him off!' And she nosed the bright bay at her feet.

The bay raised his head sleepily, but, seeing strangers, he became wide awake and struggled to his feet.

'A fine intelligent head,' Bel Bel said. 'What do you call him?'

'Storm,' Mirri answered. 'He was born in the worst of the weather, two nights ago. And yours?'

'Thowra, for the wind. He was born then too. They will be great mates for a year or so,' and both mothers nodded wisely, for was it not the way of the wild horses that the young colts should run together, after they left their dams, until they had reached the age and strength to fight for a mare or two of their own and start their own herd.

Storm and Thowra sniffed at each other curiously and then both turned back to their mothers for a drink.

ELYNE MITCHELL was born in Melbourne on 30 December 1913. Her father, General Sir Harry Chauvel, Commander of the Australian Light Horse in the First World War, taught her to ride. Elyne loved and understood horses from when she was very young. In 1935 she married Thomas Mitchell and moved to Towong Hill in the Upper Murray Valley, facing the Snowy Mountains. *The Silver Brumby*, written for the eldest of her four children and first published in 1958, began her internationally famous, twelve-book series. Elyne Mitchell died in March 2002 at the age of 88 years. Her legacy continues in the stories she created of Thowra and the other High Country brumbies.

Blinky Finds a New Home

EXCERPT FROM *THE ADVENTURES OF BLINKY BILL*

DOROTHY WALL

MRS BEAR climbed down the tree, with Blinky following close behind, and went to another tree where they had a good meal of young leaves and tender shoots.

'Why are we eating so much?' Blinky inquired.

'We are going away, dear,' Mrs Bear replied. 'We must find a tree farther in the bush where those men with guns can't come, and as we may be a long time in finding a suitable home, these leaves will keep us from feeling hungry.'

Together the mother and her cub slowly climbed down the tree, and great was their surprise to find Angelina Wallaby waiting for them.

'Where are you going, Mrs Bear?' she asked.

'Far into the bush with Blinky, away from the man with his gun,' Mrs Bear replied.

'What will I do?' asked Angelina. 'I shall miss Blinky terribly.' And her big eyes filled with tears.

'Come with us,' grunted Blinky.

'Oh, that would be splendid,' said Angelina. 'I know a gum-tree far away with a baby in it just like Blinky. Blinky can crawl up on my back when his legs are tired, and I'll carry him along – you too, Mrs Bear, if you feel the journey too long.'

Thanking her, the three started away. Mrs Bear turned and gave one sorrowful look at the tree that had been their home for so long. It had been a kind tree, sheltering them through all weathers and feeding them every day of the year, but not strong enough to protect them from tragedy.

After travelling for a mile or more the bears began to feel very tired, as they were not used to walking along the ground. Very rarely they leave the branches of the trees; occasionally one will climb down to feed on some vegetation in the grass; but they feel very strange having to use their four legs to walk with. It is so different to sitting on a limb of a tree, hind paws firmly grasping the branch while the two front paws are busily pulling down tender leaves to their mouths. So it was no wonder when Mrs Koala and Blinky began to limp.

'Let us rest here under this bush,' said Angelina, hopping up to a thick scrubby tree. 'We can have a sleep, and when the moon is up we will go on.'

In the cool shade they slept until the sun went down, then waking up, and feeling very hungry, Mrs Koala and Blinky climbed a sapling. Blinky rushed ahead as they neared the top and stuffed his mouth as full as full.

'Don't gobble,' said Mrs Bear, cuffing his ear.

'They're so juicy,' said young Blinky, as he peered over the branch and threw a few leaves down to Angelina.

'They are nice,' said Angelina, as she munched them ever so gently. 'I have never tasted these leaves before; but we must not stop here any longer. This is strange country, and we have a long way to go.'

'I don't want to go,' wailed Blinky, 'I'm tired.'

'Both of you hop on my back and we'll be there in no time. I can leap along in the moonlight like a kangaroo.'

After some arguing over the matter, Mrs Bear and Blinky climbed on her back, and away they went. It was great fun. Flop, flop, flop, through the grass, ducking their heads to miss the branches and twigs of low-growing trees, and then racing along through open country.

Many a rabbit looked up in surprise from his supper-table to see the strange sight, and possums screeched in the branches as they looked down at some new kind of wallaby, as they thought. At last, breathless and tired, Angelina stopped at the foot of a tall, straight gum-tree. Silver white it stood in the moonlight with branches spread far up in the sky.

'Here is your new home,' said Angelina.

'How beautiful,' murmured Mrs Bear, as she and Blinky crawled down their friend's back.

'It is safe, and you will be very happy here and Blinky will have a playmate.' Angelina flopped on the grass, her long legs sprawled out, and she panted loudly.

'Where are you going to live?' Mrs Bear inquired. 'We want you to live near us, please.'

'I'm going to live just round the corner,' said Angelina. 'I have a friend waiting for me.'

'Is she a relation?' asked Mrs Bear kindly.

'No!' replied Angelina. 'She is a he!' And, blushing, she looked very slowly down at her paws; then suddenly turned and hopped away.

'Dear, dear,' grunted Mrs Bear, 'the world is full of surprises.'

DOROTHY WALL, writer and illustrator, was born on 12 January 1894 at Wellington, in New Zealand. She came to Australia in 1914, settling in Sydney, and began work as a free-lance artist. In 1933 she moved to the Blue Mountains with her son Peter, where she wrote and illustrated her *Blinky Bill* series. *The Complete Adventures of Blinky Bill*, a collection of her stories about the mischievous young koala, was first published in 1939. Dorothy died from pneumonia in 1942, when she was 48.

Gran's Beaut Ute

MARGARET CLARK

MY GRAN has this fantastic farm. There are some beef cattle, some chooks and there's an old cattle dog called Bob. Dad and Mum don't like the farm. But I love it!

Best of all, there's this ute that Gran calls her Beaut Ute. Dad says it's a heap of junk. But I know it's not.

Inside, there's a little knob to turn on the windscreen wipers. There's another to turn on the lights. On the floor, there's a fat button that Gran can push with her foot when she has to dip her lights. The gears are on the side of the steering column. And there are funny little windows like triangles next to the main ones.

And best of all, the old ute can carry almost anything!

I think it's beaut, just like Gran does!

Mum says it's an old rust bucket. She says it smells of spilt petrol. And stale socks. And cow manure. But I love the smell of Gran's old ute. I think it smells of adventures. I know about the adventures because they always happen to me and Gran, especially on school holidays. And this is one of the best adventures ever!

I was staying at Gran's farm one time and a young guy called Tim was there too, helping her out with the chores in return for food and board.

'Just as well you're both here,' said Gran, 'because in two days' time it's the Country Show.'

Gran had entered Chappie, her brown and white prize bull, in the Best Behaved Bull section. He's won it for three years in a row because he's very quiet and calm.

This year there was a new section at the Show. It was called the Best Beaut Ute.

'I think I'll enter, just for fun,' said Gran.

I looked at the ute. One door had holes in it where a steer had gored it with its horns. The other door had a big scratch where Gran had gone too close to a fence. The front bumper bar was squashed where Gran had run into a tree. The back bumper bar had a dent where she'd backed into a stump. The paint was faded and shabby. There was rust along the tailgate.

'She's got no hope of winning,' Tim whispered to me.

'But we have to try,' I said. 'Gran loves her old ute and so do I.'

We didn't have any special car shampoo to wash the ute, so we used Sweet Roses shampoo. We dried it with a hair dryer. Then we put on some polish and rubbed hard till it shone. Sort of! And Tim put black stuff that Gran used to clean the stove on the tyres. The old ute looked much better.

'It still stinks,' said Tim.

So we cleaned out all the bits of straw. And mud. And manure. And lolly papers.

We shook the mats. I put an Odour Eater under the seat.

'Hmm,' said Tim as he looked at the ute. 'Well, we did our best.'

Finally, the day of the Country Show arrived. Bob herded Chappie towards the ute. Gran got the ramp in position.

'She's not going to put that wild bull in there, is she?' Tim muttered to me.

'Chappie always rides in the ute. It's a big adventure for him.'

'But –'

'It's a very strong ute and Chappie's a small, quiet bull,' Gran said. 'He'll just stand in there like a statue!'

Chappie walked up the ramp. Gran tied his nose ring to the chain and she tied side ropes on him to keep him steady. Then she slid in the ramp and put up the tailgate.

'You two did a lovely job on the old ute. It will win first prize for sure,' said Gran happily. 'Off we go!'

There wasn't much room in the front and Chappie had all the space in the back. Bob had to sit on the floor. I turned round to check on Chappie. Was he all right? I couldn't see. His hot bull's breath had steamed up the window. It wasn't far to the Country Show. But Chappie couldn't wait. When we arrived, he'd done a big, smelly plop all over the floor of the nice, clean ute!

But the real trouble started when he went into his pen. He didn't like the bull next to him, and he wanted to meet the pretty cow in the other stall. He was not quiet at all! He bellowed and roared and bucked. He tried to smash down his stall, so he was disqualified from the contest!

But Tim and I didn't know that. We were busy cleaning the back of the ute.

'Phew. What a stink!' said Tim.

I knew that even a tonne of Odour Eaters wouldn't fix this problem!

Then Gran came back. She was upset that happy Chappie had turned into a raging bull.

'Never mind,' I said. 'You can still go in the Best Ute contest.'

Utes had come from all over the country. The prizes were for Best Beaut Feral Ute, Best Beaut Old Ute, Best Beaut Ute Sound System, Best Beaut Ute With The Most Stickers, and Best Beaut Unusual Ute.

Most of the utes were shiny and new. Even the old ones were polished and clean.

'I suppose we could win the Best Beaut Feral Ute,' said Tim.

'Maybe we should have left Chappie's plop in the back.'

I thought our only hope was Best Beaut Unusual Ute!

One of the judges came to Gran's ute.

He ran his fingers over the holes in the door.

'A steer gored it,' I said.

He looked at the squashed front bumper bar. 'Gran hit a tree,' I said.

He walked round the other side. 'Gran hit a gate post,' I explained.

He frowned at the dent in the rear bumper bar.

'Gran backed into a stump,' I said. 'This ute's had a lot of adventures.'

'I can see that,' said the judge. He went to the next ute.

Gran had gone to check on Chappie. When she came back, she said that Chappie was still staring at the cow. He'd never done that before.

'What did the judge say?' she asked.

'I think he loves your beaut ute,' I said quickly.

The judges put their heads together. It took a while. Then they announced the winners.

A man from Glue Glue won the Best Beaut Ute With The Most Stickers.

A lady from Echo Point won the Best Beaut Ute Best Sound System.

And a man from Wild Dog Creek won the Best Beaut Feral Ute.

The prize for the Best Beaut Old Ute went to a lady and man team from the U Beaut Ute business in the next town.

There was only one prize left: the Best Unusual Beaut Ute. And it went to Melvin O'Weird from Strangetown.

I felt like yelling, 'Boo! Boo!' Couldn't those silly judges see that Gran's beaut ute was the best?

Suddenly, the chief judge held up his hand. What was going on?

'We have added a special award,' he said. 'It's for the Best Beaut Adventure Ute. This old ute has been gored by a bull. It's crashed into trees. And stumps. And gate posts. It's got faded paintwork. It's got rust along the tailgate. It's certainly had a lot of adventures. So, the winner is – Gran's Beaut Ute!'

We all clapped as Gran went to get the First Prize Blue Ribbon.

The owner of the Best Beaut Ute With The Most Stickers even gave Gran a sticker for her ute. It said REV IT UP, BABY.

Chappie didn't come back in the ute. Gran said he was too frisky. He was going for a short stay to play with some nice young heifers on the next farm. Gran didn't mind, though, because she'd won first prize anyway.

The old beaut ute was a winner!

MARGARET CLARK was born in 1945 and has worked as a teacher, a university lecturer and at the Geelong Centre for Alcohol and Drug Dependency before writing full-time. Her novels for older readers include *The Big Chocolate Bar, Fat Chance, Hot or What, Kiss and Make Up, Famous for Five Minutes* and a trilogy about the Studley family: *Hold my Hand or Else!, Living with Leanne* and *Pulling the Moves.* Her *Secret Girls' Stuff, More Secret Girls' Stuff,* and *What to do When Life Sucks* have become best-sellers.

Margaret lives in Geelong and enjoys reading, sailing and walks with her dog. Visit her website at www.margaretclark.com.au

Ms White's Garden

VASHTI FARRER

FLORENCE WHITE had green thumbs. Well, actually they were pink, but when I say they were green I mean she was good at gardening. She loved her garden. It was her greatest joy, and she had spent years getting it just the way she wanted. But now that it *was* just as she wanted it, she was too worn out to work in it any more.

All those years of digging flower beds, lugging bags of manure, moving tree stumps and mowing the lawns had strained her back. What's more, she had housemaid's knee from all that kneeling to weed her garden, and student's elbow from years spent carrying pots and watering cans. As for the rest of her joints, well, they were all a bit floppy and soggy. Now, all she could do was lie in a hammock each day and watch the grass grow.

The trouble was, Florence wasn't getting any younger. In fact, she was quite old. And she was finding it harder and harder to look after her garden.

'Why don't you get a gardener?' the neighbours suggested.

'Oh, no, I couldn't do that,' she said. 'No one would work in the garden as hard as I have, because no one would love it as much as I do.'

So she went on lying on her back in her hammock and watching the grass.

But in the end, the garden started to look overgrown and unkempt, even *neglected*. Whenever the neighbours passed, they tut-tutted. 'What a pity, such a lovely garden, what a shame to let it get run down.'

One day, as the neighbours passed and said these things, Florence overheard them. 'I've got to do something,' she thought. 'The neighbours are beginning to talk.'

So she climbed out of the hammock and went inside. She opened the newspaper and looked in the *Ads for Gardeners* column. 'These are no good,' she said. 'There isn't one I'd trust to take care of my beloved garden. I'll just have to go downtown and find one.'

She got in her car and drove down to the local CES, or 'Can Employ Some' shop.

There, all round the walls, were noticeboards with ads for jobs – and sitting underneath one of the noticeboards she saw six little men.

'Who are you?' asked Florence.

'Gnomes,' said the first.

'Don't you mean dwarfs?'

'No, Ma'am, gnomes, as in garden,' said the second.

'Shouldn't there be seven of you?'

'There were,' said a third, 'until Gawain got a job as a land-scape gardener.'

'And do the rest of you know anything about gardening?'

'Know anything about . . . ? You hear that, boys! Listen,

lady, that's why we're called *garden* gnomes. We're in the business of gardening.'

'But if you're so good, how come you haven't got jobs already?' she asked.

'Because most people only want *one* gardener,' said the fourth gnome. 'And after Gawain split, we decided to stick together. *Take One, Take All,* that's our new motto.'

'I'm not sure,' said Florence, frowning.

'Look, what sort of garden do you have?' said the fifth. 'A couple of pot plants on a windowsill? Geraniums? Herbs, maybe?'

'Oh no,' said Florence. 'It's a *big* garden. With rolling lawns and big wide flower beds and lovely shady trees and lots of quiet restful spots. The trouble is, it's too big for me to manage any more, and it's beginning to look run down.'

'Well, there you are then,' said the sixth. 'What you need is a team effort, not someone to come in once a month and dribble a hose on something. We move in. Live in, in fact. And we offer on-the-spot, twenty-four-hour service. In no time at all, yours will be the best-looking garden in the street.'

'Oh, but I don't want the neighbours knowing I've had to get help,' said Florence. 'You see, I've done it all myself so far.'

'We quite understand,' said the gnomes. 'We're very discreet.'

'Yes, we only work at night.'

'You see, we're nocturnal. We knock off during the day.'

'We may stand around in the garden a lot, but actually we're getting a bit of shut-eye before starting again.'

'We do all the popular poses too. Let's see . . . we do *Gnome Holding a Flowerpot, Gnome Carrying a Sack on His Shoulder, Gnome Sitting on a Toadstool* and *Gnome Asleep over a Fishing Rod.*'

'And we're very reasonably priced, if you take us as a job lot.'

'Very well then, I will!' said Florence.

'Excellent!' said the gnomes.

'But you will promise to take care of my garden, won't you?'

'As if it were our own. Now let's introduce ourselves: Garth, Gerald, Gideon, Gilbert, Godwin and Giles, at your service.'

'And I'm Florence,' said Ms White.

An hour later, the neighbours saw Florence unloading her car.

'That's odd,' they said. 'Fancy putting gnomes in when the garden's so run down.'

But within a week the garden was no longer run down. It was splendid – in fact, magnificent – by far the best garden in the street.

The gnomes had done all the digging, weeding, pruning, mowing, raking and hoeing to get it back into shape. Not only that, they had done all the housework. Garth had done the dusting, Gerald the vacuuming, Gideon had made the bed, Gilbert had done the washing, Godwin the ironing, and Giles had taken out the garbage.

Florence found she didn't have to do a thing, and her garden was looking lovelier than ever.

The neighbours had no idea how she managed it. That remained a secret between Flo White and her Garden Gnomes.

VASHTI FARRER writes short stories for adults, and plays, poetry and stories for primary and secondary schools. She is a regular contributor to the *School Magazine*. Vashti is best known for her historical novels for young readers, which include *Escape to Eaglehawk*, *Eureka Gold* and *Ned's Kang-u-roo*. One of her books in the *My Story* series, *Plagues and Federation – the Diary of Kitty Barnes*, is set in the Rocks area of Sydney in 1900. Vashti loves theatre, acting, history, archaeology and unusual characters.

Introducing the Very Naughty Mother

EXCERPT FROM *THE VERY NAUGHTY MOTHER GOES GREEN*

GRETEL KILLEEN

SOME DAYS are sunny, some days it pours.
Some shoes fit, some make your feet sore,
Some tv is funny, some tv's a bore
and
Most mothers are perfect.
But every now and then one comes along who is very,

very,

very,

very

naughty.

The Very Naughty Mother would not get out of bed and lay under the blankets, picking her nose and eating the snot.

'Time to get up,' called her son, Zed, as he knocked gently on his mother's bedroom door.

But the Very Naughty Mother did not reply, and instead put

one finger in each ear and placed a fluffy purple pillow over her head.

'Come on, Mummy,' called Pink, Zed's little sister, as she stood at the bottom of the stairs, wiping her hands on her enormous mother's-sized apron. 'I've made a yummy breakfast for you and if you don't hurry up and get dressed you'll be really late for work.'

But the Very Naughty Mother did not reply and started to snore like a little pig instead.

'Wake up, Mum,' called Zed once again as he tap-tap-tapped upon the bedroom door.

But the tap-tap-tapping did not stop the Very Naughty Mother's snores and actually, miraculously, only made the Very Naughty Mother want to snore some more!

So Zed stopped tap-tapping on the door and tapped his foot on the floor while he wondered what to do. Should he beg, should he yell, or should he just go into the bedroom and tickle his mother until she woke up with the giggles?

Well, after some thought, Zed realised that he couldn't enter the room because the Very Naughty Mother had put a sign on her door that said

TRESPASSERS WILL BE PROSECUTED

and he wanted to respect his mother's individuality and personal space. (And besides, the last time Zed entered his mother's room without permission, a custard pie boobytrap landed on his head.)

'It's time to get up and get ready,' said Zed through the keyhole. 'So wake up, stop that snoring, and hop right out of bed.' But the Very Naughty Mother did the opposite of 'stop' and let out a mighty super-dooper snore instead.

SNORE

'I suspect she's faking it,' said Pink who had joined Zed at their mother's bedroom door. 'Don't you remember she did this only last week when we told her she had to go tidy her room, and she stood perfectly still with her eyes wide open, and said that she couldn't possibly tidy a thing because she was fast asleep. So my guess is,' continued Pink, 'that the longer we let her continue with this the louder her snores are going to roar.'

And with that, just like a magic spell had been cast, the Very Naughty Mother let out a mighty . . .

ROAR!

'We know you're pretending,' called Zed through the door. 'We know you're pretending to doze, because no one could possibly sleep through snores that sound like a piglet is stuck up their nose.'

'Yes, get out of bed,' said Pink with a blink, 'cos if you don't you'll have to be punished with . . . um . . . no television for a whole week.'

Well it might come as a shock but the snoring stopped and for a moment the Very Naughty Mother was as quiet as absolute nothingness.

'Oh,' said Zed, 'maybe she really has gone to sleep and you and I were just in a muddle.'

'Yes,' replied Pink, 'that's what I tend to think, so let's enter her room without making a sound and wake her up with a gigantic cuddle.'

But the Very Naughty Mother had been listening at the keyhole and before you could say 'haleely bot bing', had shoved a huge lion against the door to stop anyone from entering.

(It was, of course, the huge stuffed lion that the King of Tittywa had given the Very Naughty Mother as a reward for climbing the mountains of Hajah-baj while wearing a crown and a tutu.)

The lion was enormous, so even after all Zed's huffing and

puffing the door would only open wide enough for a worm or a tadpole to slither through. And this was a problem, because the time was slipping away and the Very Naughty Mother's boss had told her that if she was late one more time this week then he had no choice but to fire her. (No, not out of a cannon.)

'They can't fire me,' called the Very Naughty Mother from her room, forgetting that she was asleep. 'The door's jammed tight and I can't get out.' And she began to weep (or at least try hard to pretend to).

Oh yes, the Very Naughty Mother started to sob, like a blob that had been bitten by a blubber.

Blob, blub,
blib-bloober.
Blob, blub,
blib-bloober.

After a while the Very Naughty Mother realised that she didn't sound like she was crying at all and instead sounded like a leaking tap. So she increased the volume of her blobs, whispered her blibs and added some 'ooooooooooooo's' to her bloobers. But she still didn't sound like she was crying and instead sounded like a drunk Martian. So the Very Naughty Mother tried even harder. Faster, harder, louder, softer, with more 'ooooooooooooooooooooooooooooooooooo ooooooooooooooooooooooooooooooooooooooooooooooooooooooo ooooooooooooooo's' and lots more blubs. In fact she tried so hard to sound like she was crying that after just forty-three seconds her nose went red, her ears went green, her face went the shape of a potato and the Very Naughty Mother got a very, very bad headache.

And that's when she really started to cry.

'Don't worry,' said Pink urgently through the keyhole. 'You won't get fired, Mummy, because we'll find another way to get into the room and we'll have you out in a jiffy. But in the meantime I suggest you get dressed so you're ready to leave with a zoom.' (Not a broom or a goon or a va-va-va-voom, but a zoom, which is the fastest way to leave anywhere unless you have a supersonic rocket that is painted yellow.)

Well, I can honestly say that the Very Naughty Mother did begin to get dressed because she put her high-heel shoes on with her pyjamas. But then she stopped dressing right there and then, and instead carefully checked the door was still blocked, gently stood on her bed and began ever so quietly to jump up and down like a jack-in-a-box.

Up and down she went, up and down, up and down, while the children gave up on opening the door and ran around the side of the house to climb up to their mother's bedroom window. And all the while the Very Naughty Mother continued to bounce until she accidentally jumped right off the bed and landed with a thump on the floor.

And that's when the Very Naughty Mother looked up, as she lay flat on the floor with her eyes rolled backwards, and saw that two little faces were peering through the bedroom window with their noses squashed flat against the glass. And they didn't look very happy.

UH-OH, BUSTED!!!!!!!!!!

So what do you think the Very Naughty Mother did? Do you think she opened the window to let her children in? Do you think she said, 'Oh, I was just jumping up to see if you were coming to rescue me,' or do you think she said, 'Oh, thank heavens you're here, I've just been sword-fighting an invisible monster'? Well, no, she didn't. She did not say any of these fab things. No, diddle-diddle diddle-do, she just got up from the floor, jump-boinged to the window and quickly closed the curtains.

'She closed the curtains,' said Zed to Pink as they hung from the windowsill. 'Our mother is really very rude. In fact we should smack her bottom.'

'There's no point in even trying,' said Pink, 'because our hands are so small and her bum is so big.'

'I heard that!' yelled the Very Naughty Mother as she continued to bounce up and down.

'Well,' said Zed, 'then hear me tell you to stop jumping on the bed.'

'I want to stop,' said the Very Naughty Mother, 'but the bump off the bed, has sent a note to my head, saying I have to keep jumping instead.'

Well Pink believed her very naughty mother because she loved her enormously and only wanted the very best for her mum. And although Zed didn't really believe his mother, he couldn't smack her bottom because it was too enormous and he couldn't send her to her room because she was already there, so he decided to agree with Pink and be nice to their mum and encourage her to go off to work.

So the next thing you know Pink kindly asked her mother to open the curtain and then open the window so that the two children could climb into their mother's room.

And the Very Naughty Mother said that she would open the curtain and she would open the window. But then, I guess, the bump on her head made her forget and she went to the bed and started bouncing instead.

Oh yes, she bounced, just a little bit at first, and then a great big bit higher. And then she bounced a little bit more, and a little bit more, until she was bouncing like a truly professional bouncer who might bounce in a circus called Bits That Bounce a Bit.

Bounce, bounce, bounce, she bounced, and then she

bounce, bounce, bounced some more. She bounced with a
boing, thump, boing thump, boing and even screamed 'Yehah!'
with joy.

'Yehaaaaaaaaaaaaaaaaaaaaaaaaaaaaaaaaaaaaaaaaaaaaaaaaaaa
aaaaaaaaaah!'

Until suddenly there was a whoop

and a twang

and then a creak,

and a crack

and a great splack, splick, oomph

and the Very Naughty Mother fell through the mattress, the
bedbase and the floorboards, and only stopped plummeting to
the kitchen underneath because her bottom got caught in the
ceiling.

GRETEL KILLEEN started her career as a stand-up comic. She appears reguarlarly on
national television and radio, and hosts the *Big Brother* shows. Her books include the *My
Sister's* and *Very Naughty Mother* series, plus the Fleur Trotter – *My Life* – series. Gretel
is currently running around like a headless chook raising her son and daughter and
preparing several of her works for TV and film.

Slam Jam Sam

MIKE DUMBLETON

BRILLIANT! Sam had the basketball court to herself. There were no big kids hanging off the ring and yelling at her to get out of the way.

She was determined to shoot ten baskets in a row.

Six ... seven ... eight ... CLUNK.

Blast! It was always the same. She could never get to ten.

As she gathered the ball from the side of the court something glinted in the dirt. She reached out to touch it and was instantly disappointed. It wasn't anything valuable. It was an old drink can, buried in the ground. But just to check, she rubbed away some of the dirt.

Swi i i i sh! A sound like an opening drink can swept through the air. A strange shape formed above the can and hovered in front of her.

It had a head like a basketball, and a cap swivelled backwards.

'I am the Slam Jam Genie.'

'Wicked!' exclaimed Sam. Then, before the Genie could say anything else, Sam added, 'I've got three wishes, haven't I?'

'Great!' said the Genie. 'I've been stuck in that dark drink can just dying to burst out and tell someone they've got three wishes. Then, when it finally happens, you ruin it for me.'

The Genie looked upset, but Sam was in too much of a hurry to notice.

'I wish I could score ten baskets in a row.'

◆

Six . . . seven . . . eight . . . nine

Sam fixed her eyes on the basket, ready to take the final shot. The ball left her fingertips and she held her breath.

It sailed above the basket, crashed onto the ring and rebounded higher than the backboard. Then swoosh! – it plunged straight through the net.

'Yessss!' With both arms stretching to the sky, Sam gave the Genie a huge grin. 'Thanks.'

'Don't thank me,' said the Genie, shaking his head. 'I didn't do anything. You scored those ten baskets all by yourself.'

'Yeah, sure,' laughed Sam.

'It's true,' insisted the Genie. 'Wishes don't come true until I say, "Your wish is granted", and you didn't give me time to say it.'

Sam beamed. This was the greatest day ever. She'd just shot ten baskets in a row and she still had three wishes left.

'Let's try the wishes thing again,' said Sam. 'Start from where you come out of the drink can, and I'll see if I can get it right this time.'

◆

'I am the Slam Jam Genie,' announced the Genie for the second time. Sam said nothing.

'You have three wishes,' continued the Genie, looking pleased. 'Now tell me, what will they be?'

'I wish I had lots of money. I wish I was a famous pop star, and I wish I could fly,' Sam exclaimed.

'Hang on, hang on,' said the Genie, shaking his head. 'You've got it all wrong again. I'm called the Slam Jam Genie because I only grant wishes to do with basketball.'

Sam thought carefully. 'I wish,' she said, with a cheeky smile broadening all over her face, 'that all my other wishes about basketball will come true.'

'Huh,' snorted the Genie. 'I suppose you think that's very clever.' Then he put his hand in his pocket and pulled out his *Everything You Ever Wanted to Know about Being a Slam Jam Genie* book. He turned to the section on 'People who wish that all their other wishes about basketball will come true'.

'There's always someone,' he read out, 'who tries to get extra wishes. But nobody gets more than three. Just tell them their wish has been granted. All their other wishes will come true. All two of them!'

'Oh no!' Sam groaned. 'Now I've wasted my first wish.'

'That's what you get for being greedy,' confirmed the Genie.

'I wish I could do a slam dunk,' said Sam.

'That's more like it.' The Genie nodded. Then he declared importantly, 'Your wish is granted.'

Sam picked up the basketball. She took two steps towards the basket and jumped into the air. Her feet left the ground and she kept going higher and higher.

She waited until she was past the net, above the ring and level with the backboard. Then she slammed the ball into the basket. Her fingers curled around the metal rim and she swung from the ring briefly before dropping to the ground.

'I did it!' she yelled triumphantly.

'I've got a new name for you,' laughed the Genie. 'Slam Jam Sam!'

'I wish I was the best basketballer in the world,' said Sam, making her last wish.

'Your wish is granted,' said the Genie.

Sam scored fifty baskets without missing. She dribbled the ball behind her back and through her legs at break-neck speed. Then she jammed the ball into the net, at both ends of the court, with huge slam dunks that made the whole framework shudder and shake.

'That was brilliant,' said the Genie. 'It's a pity it won't last.'

Sam looked puzzled.

'You only said you wanted to be the best basketballer in the world,' explained the Genie. 'You didn't say for how long.'

◆

Sam was shooting baskets by herself when her father called by to say that tea was ready.

The Genie had disappeared, saying he needed a good rest. He had gone to search for an empty drink can that would be hard for anyone to find.

Sam scored eight baskets then she missed and sighed loudly.

'Don't waste time sighing,' said her father. 'Think about all the shots that went in.'

Sam thought about it and smiled.

'I shot ten baskets in a row today,' she said. 'And I did it all by myself.'

'I'm sure you did,' laughed her father. 'As far as I'm concerned,' he added, 'you're the best basketballer in the world.'

Sam couldn't stop smiling as she looked around the court.

The Genie wasn't anywhere to be seen . . . but her last wish still seemed to be working.

MIKE DUMBLETON is a writer with many picture books to his credit, including *Let's Escape,* *Downsized* and *Muddled-up Farm.* Five of his books have been selected as Notable Books by the Australian Children's Book Council, and *Passing On* was shortlisted for the 2002 Book of the Year Awards. Mike was also recently awarded an Arts SA Literature Grant, by the South Australian government, to support the completion of his first young adult fiction title, *Watch Out For Jamie Joel.*

Mike's website is at www.mikedumbleton.cjb.net

The Hippolottamuss

NAN HUNT

GEOFFREY had it all planned. The box was under his bed, with some twine to tie the lid on. He had poked holes all round the box with scissors.

Thomas-Across-the-Street was happy to go. The big marmalade cat really belonged to Mr and Mrs Mason, but spent most of his time with Geoffrey because there were shrubs in the garden for him to sleep under, and Geoffrey knew just where he liked being tickled and stroked.

Under the weeping elm, in the yard where it was cool and secret, Geoffrey had told Thomas, 'Now Dad's gone, Mum and Jane and me – we have to go away from here to live in the city, you see, and the big van is coming to take all the stuff, but you can come in the car.'

Thomas yawned and purred.

When the van arrived, his mother was too busy to notice what Geoffrey was doing until she called him to get into the car. 'What's in the box?'

'Thomas-Across-the-Street.'

'You can't take him! For one thing he doesn't belong to you, he belongs to the Masons, and for another thing pets are not allowed in the unit. Hurry up and take him back.'

It wasn't the kind of farewell Geoffrey or Thomas would have liked, and Thomas was offended and disappeared quickly when he was let out of the box. In the car, Geoffrey was very quiet. He refused to cry, but the tears ran down inside him and made his stomach ache.

After the first week in the town house, when the family was settling down to their new surroundings, Geoffrey brought home the Hippolottamuss. He made a bed for it beside his own and insisted it should be fed. He was forever saying, 'Look out, you're treading on the Hippolottamuss,' or, 'You can't sit on that chair, that's where the Hippolottamuss is asleep.'

'I can't see it,' said his sister Jane. 'There's nothing there at all.'

'There is so, and he doesn't like being sat on.'

The family put up with it for a week, thinking it would go away, but the Hippolottamuss stayed.

He needed to be taken outside.

He needed the television on to keep him from being bored.

He needed 'his special space', and his own dish of water on the bathroom floor.

'It's all in your mind, Geoffrey,' said Jane. 'It's only an imaginary pet.'

'The Hippolottamuss is not a menagerie pet. He's real and he's mine and he's here.'

After a fortnight the family was desperate. The Hippolottamuss was taking over their lives. 'That beast has to go,' his mother said. 'Please, Geoffrey, take him out and lose him.'

'That would be cruel, and you told me never to be cruel to animals.'

'But he's not a real animal, Geoffrey.'

'Of course he is. He's as real as you and Jane and – and Dad.'

'That's enough, Geoffrey. He can't live here.'

But the Hippolottamuss stayed.

At last Geoffrey's mother rang up Granny, who laughed.

'I'll send Gramp over,' she said.

As soon as he arrived, Gramp went looking for Geoffrey. 'Are you going to introduce me to the Hippolottamuss?'

'Perhaps, Gramp. If he feels like it. You can come with me to where he is, if you like.'

'What's his name, Geoffrey?'

'Tom – no, Billy. Yes, Billy is his name.'

'Can you draw me a picture of him?'

'Yes, yes!' Geoffrey ran to get paper and textas.

Gramp sat on the floor and watched while he drew two orange circles, a long curly tail, and some whiskers. 'That's a good colour. I like it. He reminds me of someone I know. Don't tell me, I know! Isn't that Thomas-Across-the-Street?'

Geoffrey nodded, and suddenly he was in his gramp's lap and crying tears on the outside of his face that helped take away some of the lonely missing-Thomas-very-much ache in his inside.

NAN HUNT was born on 16 September 1918 in Bathurst, New South Wales. Her first writing appeared on the children's page of the Sydney *Sun* newspaper and the Melbourne *Leader* when she was eleven. Nan is one of Australia's best-loved authors for young readers, well known for her picture books such as *The Dove Tree*, *The Harvest Loaf* and the award-winning *Whistle Up the Chimney*. Her fiction includes *The Pow Toe*, *Phoenix* and *A Patch of Sunlight*.

'Friday' and 'Saturday'

EXCERPT FROM *PENNY POLLARD'S DIARY*
ROBIN KLEIN

FRIDAY

I am going to try very hard to catch malaria over the weekend. Poked a hole in fly-wire in my bedroom so mozzies can get in. Hope they are proper malaria kind. Also will gargle with red food colouring so throat looks like scarlet fever. *Do not want to go to school on Monday!*

Miss James said our class going to visit nursing home for senior citizens and play our recorders for them and sing daggy songs from *Sound of Music*. Put up my hand and asked why our excursion couldn't be to a racing stable instead. Miss J. gave me snaky look. (She never does to Simone who is her pet.) 'I didn't say anything about it being an excursion, Penny Pollard,' she said. 'Senior citizens are not public exhibits at the other end of a bus ride. This is for your community work project. Nobody is too young to learn service to the rest of the community.' She gave me extra snaky look meaning she didn't think I was any shining jewel as far as social work concerned. Simone put up her hand and said she'd spend all her pocket money on roses lace hankies chocolates to take to senior citizens at the nursing home. Miss J. beamed. Simone said she'd also bake a special cake and make whole lot of lavender bags trimmed with lace and ribbons as little surprise presents. (If anyone gave me a present like that I would kick them.)

I put up my hand and said, 'Can I stay back at school on Monday instead of going on that excursion?' Miss J. asked why. Told her I didn't want to visit a lot of old ladies. Told her I thought old people just plain boring and always talking about their rheumatism and asking if it's three o'clock yet because they have to take their pill. And they look creepy, like tired old trees in winter.

I told her I would not go to that nursing home and that's all there was to it and I didn't intend to discuss the matter any further!

(Didn't say last sentence out loud.)

Miss J. told me off for views on senior citizens then handed out permission forms parents have to sign or we can't leave on the bus Monday for our visit to that dumb place.

Hid my form in gumboot when I got home.

SATURDAY

Mum met Simone's when she doing the shopping. 'Just where is that form I have to sign for the visit to the nursing home, Penny?' she said when she got back. 'You can wear your pretty pink dress Aunty Janice sent from Adelaide what do you mean yuk I will not have that dress just hanging up in the wardrobe for months not worn I don't intend to discuss the matter any further Penny how did this permission form get horse manure all over it?'

Feel sick every time I look at that pink dress from Aunty Janice (Aunty Traitor – she knew very well I wanted a stock-whip for my birthday). When the dress came I got five strong healthy-looking silverfish from the garage and put them in pocket and sealed it up with sticky-tape. But they ate sticky-tape instead of dress. (Maybe dress made them sick, too.) Also tried shrinking it while mum at work. Soaked it in mixture of Nifto Foam Carpet Cleaner, Superspeed Pot Powder, Anti-Dandruff Shampoo and Dynamo Car Wash. That yuk dress must be made of special TNT-proof laboratory-tested material. It came out brighter and pinker than ever and didn't even need ironing.

This afternoon went over to dairy and asked the man could I ride one of the horses and he said like he always does, 'Shove off, kid.'

Came home. Gargled with red food colouring and showed throat to mum, fainting at the same time. She said get up off the floor stop being silly go clean up that red food colouring mess in the kitchen sink.

Sorted out my 350 swap-cards into which has most pointy ears, longest tail, nicest face. No one at school likes my swap-card collection except me. Everyone says ace ripper when they see the big box full of cards, but after they look through first fifty and see they're all horses, they get mad and hand them back.

ROBIN KLEIN was born on 28 February 1936 in Kempsey, New South Wales, one of nine children. She left school at the age of fifteen and worked as a library assistant, teacher, telephonist, craft worker and nurse. She married and had four children and started to write seriously in the late 1970s. She became a full-time writer in 1981. Her best-selling books include *Penny Pollard's Diary* (1983), the first of a series, *Hating Alison Ashley* (1984), *The Enemies* (1984) and *Birk the Berserker* (1987). Robin has received a number of prestigious awards, including the 1991 Dromkeen Medal. She lives in Melbourne.

Moving On

MAGGIE HAMILTON

IT WAS LATE at night and at last Mick and Jodie and Mum and Dad had gone. Jack hated to see them leave, yet part of him was glad to be alone. For months he'd been getting worse. Not that anyone had said anything. They didn't need to. He could tell by the expressions on their faces what they were thinking.

The pain was back again. It shot through his body, twisting and curling up his spine and blossoming out in all directions. Then, as the spasm faded, he relaxed, his body limp with exhaustion.

Mmmm . . . his room was quiet now – deliciously quiet.

Ever since he'd got sick he loved being quiet, but before he'd the chance to enjoy a bit of peace the pain returned. Jack squeezed his eyes tight, waiting, praying for the worst to pass. Then when he thought he couldn't bear it any more, the pain dissolved and his mind was free again. It was only as he stared out beyond the tiny pool of light that encircled him that he realised he was worn out.

After trying for so long to be brave it was a relief to get to this point. Yes, that was it – relief. He thought he'd feel scared or angry even, but he wasn't. The strangest thing was that he couldn't even remember what life had been like before he'd got sick.

He wished the others were still there though – just for a bit – just so he wouldn't be alone.

Alone . . .

He didn't like the thought of being . . .

There was a sudden noise somewhere overhead. It reminded him of his pet mice – it made him smile. *Hey!* Someone was stroking his forehead. It felt great, really great. As his eyes flew open he'd expected to see one of the nurses, or Mum as she'd often come back to sit with him when the others were asleep, but there was no one there.

Pity . . .

Then as he was drawn back once more into the sea of pain Jack thought he must've imagined there was someone there, until it happened again. The same warm hand across his damp forehead, then down the side of his ice-cold cheek.

This time when Jack opened his eyes, there standing by the bed was a kid about his own age with bleached blond hair and a gaze that dove deep inside him – there was a kid who saw his pain and frustration and noted it without comment, without pity.

'Are you ready then?'

No words were spoken, but Jack heard them all the same.

Was he ready?

Yeah, he was ready to go now, right now, without any tears or long farewells. In fact he quite liked the idea of slipping away while the others were sleeping. No sooner was the thought loosed than he found himself drifting up through the grainy darkness towards the ceiling. Up and up he spiralled until he could see his whole room and the corridor and all the rooms adjoining his.

So, this was what it was like to be . . . *dead* . . .

Dead?

But this wasn't dead, it was just different and after not being able to move around for months it was cool, really cool and yet kind of normal. Unable to take it all in Jack spun round and there, directly below him, lay his body. He couldn't believe how small it looked carefully tucked up in between the stiff white sheets. It was almost as if it wasn't part of him, or at least not any more.

The sudden scream of the monitor sliced through the silence. Jack watched as doctors and nurses made a dash for his room. It was great that they cared, really great. In no time they were working on him like fury, but he didn't want to go back. Not now.

Then in less than a heartbeat the hospital had vanished. Jack found himself in a tunnel – in a warm dark kind of womb-like place. Standing right next to him was the kid who'd been by his bed. Way ahead was a pinprick of light. Before he'd time to ask questions Jack was hurtling alongside him through the darkness towards the expanding light. Faster and faster they sped. The wind caressed Jack's cheeks and arms as he went.

Strange. They were speeding along, but it took no effort at all.

Then when he least expected it, he was catapulted out of the darkness and into the light – light that was bright and yet gentle, so very gentle. His friend waved goodbye and was gone. As Jack went to take a look around, there waiting for him was Nan in her slippers and hand-knitted cardie. There too were Danny and Chris who'd drowned in the creek the previous summer. And there was Scavenger, the best dog in the world. It was kind of weird because everyone and everything seemed to be made of light, but then when Jack looked down he could see light emanating from his body – from the pores of his skin even.

The whole experience was awesome.

Time slid away. Before Jack knew it, the funeral – his funeral – was over. He was buried in an old cemetery on the top of a hill just out of town. He didn't spend much time hanging around there, but he did like the outlook. When he wasn't busy learning or exploring he liked to wander back to see how everyone was getting on.

Dad looked a whole lot older and sadder than before. He'd lost most of his hair, which didn't help. On the surface Mick and Jodie were okay, but inside they were devastated by his departure. It made Jack sad to see them like that because he was fine. In fact he was more than fine – he was having the time of his life.

Mum had kept his room just like he'd left it, except it was a heap tidier. He'd have liked to have told her that it wasn't things that kept people together, but she wouldn't have understood. Every week when she'd finished the shopping, she'd stop off at the local Catholic church to light a candle for him – not that she was a Catholic or anything really. Jack didn't mind though, because every time someone said or did something kind it made him feel warm all over.

A year or two slipped by when Jack found out that Jodie had finished the sculpture she'd been working on for what seemed like forever. Everyone seemed to like it and said it would look good above his headstone, which was kind of neat. It would have been easy to take a look at what she'd been up to, but Jack decided it was better as a surprise.

When the big day arrived to put Jodie's sculpture in place, Dad wrapped up the whole thing in some old blankets. Then, with the help of a couple of mates, he hauled it into the back of their old ute and drove it up to the cemetery. It took them ages to get the statue out of the ute and in place. Jodie was so worried they'd drop it that she couldn't even look until they were done, but when she did, she'd a smile from ear to ear.

Then when Jack moved forward to check it all out he was blown away. Jodie had carved him an angel – a life-size angel with wings and everything. It was brilliant, but it was the face of the angel that took his breath away. There, on that lone hillside, watching over the worn-out part of him stood his friend – the one who had taken him away from the hospital. Jodie had captured his shock of blond hair and his eyes and everything in perfect detail.

How, he wondered, did Jodie know about his friend? How could she have known?

But then as he studied the angel Jack realised that where Jodie had got the inspiration for her stone angel didn't matter. Not now.

All his life he'd wanted to be someone – to do something magic. Now he realised what mattered most was that time and space didn't alter how people felt about each other – that was the best kind of magic.

MAGGIE HAMILTON was born at home in a cottage in the north of England. She grew up on the edge of the moors, where the old stories were kept alive. From an early age Maggie was taken to the local graveyard to tend the graves of her relatives, and there she learnt their stories. She now lives in an old terrace house in inner-city Sydney with her husband Derek and a lively black and white cat. One of Maggie's favourite pastimes is to wander through old graveyards. She loves to read the inscriptions on the gravestones, and to imagine the kind of life the person who is buried there might have had.

The Hairyman

EXCERPT FROM *MY GIRRAGUNDJI*
MEME MCDONALD & BOORI MONTY PRYOR

THERE'S a bad spirit in our house. The Hairyman.

Aunty Lil's got a good hairyman in her house. He plays tricks on her like pinching her cup of tea and that, but it's all in fun. The Hairyman in our house is bad, real bad.

He's as ugly as ugly gets and he stinks. You touch this kind of hairyman and you lose your voice or choke to death or just die. That can happen. You do the wrong thing by these spirits and you can just drop dead. My cousins' uncle's brother did.

The Hairyman grabbed one of my sisters, you know. I've got seven of them. How unlucky is that? Seven sisters! He could have grabbed half a dozen of them for all I care. They sleep in the next room.

'You can't come in here. It's the girls' room!'

So what? We've got our own room. My brother Nicky sleeps across that side, and Paul and Rocco sleep head to toe in the bed on the wall.

One end of my bed is next to the louvre windows. I never sleep with my head up there. Too scared a hand will come through and grab me in my sleep.

I'm the oldest of us boys. The rest of them wouldn't be any good if the Hairyman had me. They'd be jammin' up, falling over each other trying to get out the door.

Anyway, one night the Hairyman – that's what us mob call those spirits – he grabbed my big sister by the throat. We were all chasing through the house. My big sister, Sue, thought she was gonna scare the rest of us, so she hid in the darkest room and kept real quiet. None of us could find her. Then all of a sudden we heard her screaming her lungs out. We raced in to see what had happened. She was still screaming, with her hands rubbing her neck. Nearly turned white, she had, white as a migaloo, a whitefulla.

She was crying and cursing and saying it must have been one of us boys muckin' around. But she knew it wasn't any of us. She felt those hands around her neck and they were hairy, wrinkly, yucky, old hands, like Quinkin hands – that's what the old people call those spirits.

With her screaming and us running, that Hairyman took off, but we all knew he'd be back.

I'm way too old to wet the bed, but there's no way I'm getting up to go to the gulmra, the dunny. Not down the hall, through the kitchen and all the way out the back. Not with that Hairyman in the house. It's dark out there.

I can't call out to my dad neither. I tried that one night but the voice got stuck in my neck like a fishbone. So, I lie in bed and hold my knees together tight for as long as I can. Sometimes I can't.

I'm real shame, too. This migaloo jalbu, Sharyn, smiled at me in maths today. One of those smiles that sticks to you like ripe mango. I tried to smile back. The best I could do was a sort of little chonky-apple smile, 'cause I know the truth. I'm still a bed-wetter.

I can't go to sleep. The music's turned up and the arguments have started. There's something funny about the night that makes grown-ups go stupid and call each other names. Maybe it's their way of scaring off the Hairyman. Maybe it's just the grog in them.

My mum reckons our people are the strongest in the world, but that drink there takes your strength away, she says. I can see it in some of those fullas' eyes. Like they've sprung a leak and the sea's come rushing in to fill them up. They're drowning inside with all that drink. When they start yelling, it's like they're calling out from the bottom of the dark sea.

I'm trying to make that sleep wash over me, carry me away in its arms. I'm trying not to think about the Hairyman. I'm telling myself he won't be coming round while all the noise keeps up. Mozzies are nagging at me.

The night is that long I think the sun has given up on us. But it hasn't. The day has a quiet about it like it's been called off. I stroll about when the rest of them are still sleeping, checking for dropped coins.

The rain poured down in the night. The water'll be coming up under our house. You've got to watch out for snakes this time of year.

Chicky, my littlest sister, starts to tease. 'Sharyn's got the hots for you, na na nana na!' She races back to the girls' room.

I know the others have put her up to it, I can hear that stupid giggling.

'Sharyn?!' I spit the name out like I've just swallowed a blowfly. 'You lot are sick.'

I go back to my room and dream about kissing. They reckon you just touch lips then poke your tongue out. Yuck! No wonder you have to do it with your eyes closed.

MEME MCDONALD grew up in western Queensland and now lives in Melbourne. She is an award-winning author of books for adults and younger readers. She has published eight books, five of which have been written in collaboration with Aboriginal writer, storyteller and performer Boori Monty Pryor. Visit Meme's website at www.mememcdonald.com

BOORI MONTY PRYOR is Kunggandji and Birri-gubba from north Queensland. He is a writer and performer who, together with Meme McDonald, has written five award-winning books: *Maybe Tomorrow*, *My Girragundji*, *The Binna Binna Man*, *Njunjul the Sun* and *Flytrap*. He regularly performs for school students and adults around Australia and overseas.

The Birthday Surprise

EXCERPT FROM *THE MUDDLE-HEADED WOMBAT*
RUTH PARK

THIS IS about the day Tabby Cat decided it was time for Wombat's birthday. Tabby was smart, and so was his friend the pouched mouse, but Wombat was muddle-headed. He didn't even know when his birthday was.

'It seems such a little while since the last one, Tabby dear,' said Mouse. 'Don't you remember how he stepped in his birthday cake? He was picking hundreds and thousands out of his toes for weeks.'

'No,' said Tabby, 'I've counted up on my paws, and next Saturday will be his birthday. You arrange the party, Mouse, and your handsome pussy will fix up a surprise.' Off he went to the garden shed and locked the door behind him.

Mouse was very excited. It shone up its small spectacles, put them back on its long, pink nose, and scuttled off to find Wombat, who was its best friend. Wombat was sitting in the yellow sunshine, eating a snail and being happy. He *was* surprised to find he was going to have a birthday.

'Will next Saturday be the eleventy-fifth of Remember, Mouse? Because *that's* my birthday.'

'It could be,' said sensible Mouse. 'Who can tell?'

All at once they heard the sounds of hammering and sawing from the garden shed.

'How horribubbly exciting!' cried Wombat. 'Tabby's making something. Let's go and look.'

'No, it's a secret,' explained Mouse.

'A secret from me!' grumbled Wombat, who felt that friends should never have secrets from each other. He trundled over to the shed door and gave it a kick. Then he banged it with his head. That hurt, so he became very cross.

'Open the door!' he roared.

'I won't!' squawked Tabby angrily. 'Mind your own business!'

'Tell him to open the door and let me see, Mouse!' said Wombat.

'No, I won't,' said Mouse calmly. 'You behave.'

Wombat trundled off grumpily. His feelings were hurt, so he pulled his raggy old straw hat down over his nose. He went and sat in Big Bush. The wind was blowing and the bush smelled of dead leaves and green leaves. Blue day-moths played in the grass. A frog made grating noises at the muddy edge of the creek. Soon Wombat became happy.

Meanwhile Mouse tapped at the door of the shed. Tabby wouldn't let it in. Mouse was so curious to know what Tabby's surprise was that it forgot it was a well-brought-up mouse. It kicked the door.

'Mean old cat!' cried Mouse, holding its foot.

'If you're going to talk to your poor, dear pussy like that, I won't tell you *what* the surprise is,' said Tabby, and he began to hammer very fast indeed, so that Mouse couldn't get a squeak in endways. So it went off and sat with Wombat and after a while it, too, felt happy again.

'You see, Wombat, Tabby is working on a surprise and it's for your birthday, and if you found out about it now, it wouldn't be a surprise.'

Even a muddle-headed Wombat could understand that. He was so pleased he stood on his head, waved his stout legs in the air, and made great noises of joy and excitement. Oh, how he loved birthdays and how he loved his kind Tabby Cat!

Of course, really, Tabby was longing to tell Mouse all about the surprise and when Mouse said it was sorry for kicking the door he forgave it so quickly Mouse didn't have time to finish what it was saying. Then they crept off to the shed.

And, what do you think, Tabby Cat was making Wombat a caravan. There wasn't much of it to be seen, just some boards and nails and lots of sawdust.

'Tabby,' said Mouse, 'you're wonderful.'

'I know,' said Tabby. 'Well now, Mouse, this is going to be a square, fat caravan, suitable for a Wombat.'

'With wheels?' said Mouse.

'Of course there'll be wheels. One on each corner. They'll be yellow and black, and you may help paint them.'

Mouse's nose turned pink as a sea-shell with excitement. Mouse loved to paint. But it had a question.

'How will the caravan move, Tab? Will you push it?'

Tabby could hardly believe his ears. 'Who, me? A delicate little cat like me? Of course not, silly Mouse. We will tie it to Wombat's bike, and then he'll pedal away and off we'll go.'

Mouse thought Tabby was very clever. Tabby quickly banged some timber together into a box shape. He turned it over.

'Now, Mouse, be quiet. No little words of advice or any-thing like that.'

Mouse said it wouldn't squeak a word.

Tabby fastened on the axle where the wheels would go. He slipped on the shiny metal wheels. He looked at Mouse. Mouse didn't say anything. Tabby gave a great caterwaul.

'You might have said something when I did it so beautifully. You could have said "Well done, Faithful Tabby," or something like that.'

So Mouse said it. It sighed, for it was very hard for a Mouse to know when to be quiet and when not. Suddenly it gave a little squeak of dismay. Looking through a small crack in the shed floor was a bright, brown eye. Mouse twitched its whiskers meaningly at Tabby. Tabby looked grim. They went outside the shed and around the side wall. Sticking out from under the shed was the end of a wombat. The shed was not very far off the ground, and Wombat was squashed flat on the earth like a rather plump doormat, with his back legs sticking straight out behind him.

'Some animals,' said Mouse sternly, 'are not to be trusted.' Tabby gave a loud sob. 'My surprise is spoiled,' he moaned. 'Oh, nobody loves me, everything goes wrong!'

Wombat was very ashamed when he heard Tabby crying. He wriggled out and pulled his hat down bashfully over his eyes.

'Wombat!' said Mouse. 'You wicked, wicked animal, what did you see?'

'I saw Tabby hammering away at a dear little something. Mouse, is that my present?'

Then Tabby stopped crying. He saw that Wombat really didn't know what he was making. It would be a surprise after all. Wombat promised not to peek any more. And he didn't.

Tabby finished building the caravan and Mouse painted the

wheels yellow and black like a bee's waistcoat, and sewed little white curtains for the window. It was the most beautiful caravan anyone could wish for.

When he saw it at last, Wombat couldn't believe his eyes. He looked at the door-knob, the front step, the curtains, the bunk, and the cupboards that opened and shut. He looked at the big hook which would fasten on behind his bicycle.

'It's not for me? Not treely ruly?'

'Yes, you may ride in it, and sleep in the bunk, and do anything you like with it because it's yours,' said Tabby.

'You are the best cat in the whole world even if you *are* skinny and miserabubble-looking,' said Wombat, and he gave Tabby Cat such a hug that Tabby took ten minutes to untangle himself. By then Wombat was busily digging in the garden.

'What is he looking for?' said Mouse.

'Worms, I believe. Imagine feeling hungry when he's just been given this lovely little caravan.'

In a moment Wombat came in with his hat full of worms and snails. He began to put them in the caravan cupboard. Tabby turned pale grey with shock.

'He's putting those awful snails in the cupboard! Mouse, stop him!'

'I've never had any place to put my snails,' said Wombat happily, 'and now I've got a cupboard! Oh, thank you, thank you, Tabby.'

Tabby lay down and cried quietly to himself. To think he had spent so much time working on that dear little cupboard and now it was full to the brim with snails! But Mouse sat on Tabby's chest and stroked his whiskers.

'Wombat's just being a wombat, that's all, Tabby dear. He thinks it's the best birthday present in the world! Just look at him, Tabby!'

So Tabby looked. The caravan was shaking all over as
Wombat bounced with joy. The end of his silly scrap of a tail
was sticking out the door and waggling with excitement. All
sorts of happy wombatty noises came out of that caravan.

'He has to like things in a wombatty way, I suppose,' said
Tabby. 'It's not as though he were sensible, like a cat or a mouse.'

Just then Wombat backed out of the caravan.

'Now, I'm all ready. Who's coming?'

'Coming where?' asked Tabby, wiping away his tears with
the end of his tail.

'For a pickwick! In my caravan!'

Tabby and Mouse were delighted. They loved picnics.
Quickly they packed a lunch, sardines for Tabby and some
mosquito sandwiches for Mouse. They took fishing lines and
bathing suits and woolly jumpers in case a cold wind blew.
Mouse took its knitting. It was making some woolly gloves for
itself, for next winter. And the more they prepared for the
picnic, the more it seemed like a pickwick, which is a wombat
word for a wombatty picnic, likely to turn out full of muddles.

Very soon you might have seen Wombat pedalling off on
the bike with red wheels, with the lovely caravan bumping
along behind. Mouse and Tabby were inside the caravan, and
they didn't enjoy their ride a bit. They were very pleased when
before them they saw the sea, blue as a bluebag, with white
waves riding, and fish jumping for joy into the sunshine.

The caravan stopped. Tabby crawled out and lay on the
sand.

'Oh, what a bumpy ride. Poor little delicate pussy, no one
thinks that I might faint!'

Then he whuffled at the air.

'Fish! My favourite fruit!'

He felt much better after that.

Tabby and Wombat picked out a nice flat, rocky reef to sit on. They baited their lines. As for Mouse, it brought out a small muddly piece of green knitting and said it would sit in the sun and do some useful work.

So the pickwick started.

RUTH PARK was born in Auckland, New Zealand, in 1922. She moved to Australia in 1942 and married the writer D'Arcy Niland. After their marriage the Nilands travelled through the outback of Australia for a time before settling in Surry Hills in Sydney, where they earned a living writing full-time. Ruth wrote award-winning books for both children and adults. After her husband died in 1967, she visited London before moving to Norfolk Island from 1973 to 1985. Ruth wrote *The Muddle-Headed Wombat Goes on Holiday* in 1964.

Duck's Luck

SOPHIE MASSON

QUACK . . . *Quack* . . . *Quack* . . . *Quack!*

Tina's dad always jumped when Jonathan Puddleduck quacked. 'That drake!' he said. 'That drake drives me mad!'

Tina's mum agreed. 'He makes a mess on the paving,' she said. 'And he can't even find snails. He waits for Jemima to find them all for him.'

Tina looked out at the two ducks, Jonathan and Jemima, waddling busily in the garden. Or rather, Jemima was busy. *Whoosh!* There she went, diving in among some weeds and pulling out one and two and three snails. Jonathan Puddle-duck stood by happily. He did not try to pick up any snails. Only when Jemima moved onto the next patch did he try, and looked very surprised to find there were none left.

Quack . . . *quack* . . . *quack* . . . QUACK! he said loudly, and his pointy little duck's tail wiggled as he waddled off to join his busy wife.

'See what I mean?' said Mum.

'Yes, he wouldn't find water in the sea!' agreed Dad.

'He's just being unselfish!' said Tina softly, but no one heard her.

Jonathan and Jemima walked importantly under the pergola, the breeze ruffling their feathers. Unlike the chickens, they were allowed the run of the garden and the yard, so every day, they did their tour of inspection. Jonathan stopped by the bird table, put his head on one side and stared at the lovely stained-glass-patterned rosellas who had flown in to eat their grain. *Quack?* he asked, and Jemima answered in her firm duck's voice, *Quack*, and waddled briskly on.

'He must have seen them a hundred times before, and every time he's puzzled, the silly thing!' sighed Dad.

'Daft creature!' agreed Mum.

'He's just curious,' said Tina softly, but no one heard her.

Jonathan and Jemima swam on the pond. In their gleaming, smooth white feathers, they looked just like stout, comfortable little ships as they sailed along the muddy water. Then . . . *whoosh*, down went Jemima's head, and up went her pointy little duck's tail, and then up she came with some insect she'd found in the water. But Jonathan sailed blissfully on, only to get a terrible fright when Katie the dog barked at him.

Quack . . . quack . . . quack . . . QUACK! he protested, and scrambled out of the water towards Katie, his wings flapping. Jemima took no notice at all.

'Honestly!' said Dad. 'He'd be a goner, if that was a fox.'

'Hasn't got two brain cells to rub together!' agreed Mum.

'No, he's brave!' said Tina softly, but no one heard her.

Jemima sat on a nest full of her big white eggs. Every day, she got up and splashed water on the eggs to cool them and then settled back on the nest. Jonathan watched her in alarm and waddled up and down.

Quack . . . quack . . . quack . . . QUACK! he cried, pacing around her, so that she quacked nervously and Mum had to come and chase him away.

'You're the dumbest animal that ever lived!' Mum told Jonathan furiously, locking him into the chickens' pen.

'Maybe we should get a more intelligent mate for Jemima,' said Dad thoughtfully.

'It's not his fault. He's just anxious!' said Tina loudly, but no one took any notice.

Quack . . . quack . . . quack . . . QUACK! went Jonathan the next morning, very early. *Quack . . . quack . . . quack . . .* QUACK!

'That does it!' Tina heard Dad say as he jumped out of bed.

'Best get rid of that stupid bird,' she heard Mum agree.

Tina scrambled out of bed. She pulled on her dressing-gown and ran to the door. 'Dad,' she called out anxiously, 'he's just lonely!'

But Dad, who was halfway to the chicken pen, did not hear her, so she put on her gumboots and ran outside.

Dad unhooked the door of the chicken pen and strode in to it. Tina followed him.

Quack . . . quack . . . quack . . . QUACK! they heard Jonathan exclaim.

'Right, you – ' Dad began, just as Tina called, 'Please, Dad, he just –'

And then both of them stopped as in the same moment they saw what was inside.

The chickens were all clustered up one side of their house, clucking shrilly; and there was Jonathan in the middle, quacking loudly and doing a waddling dance – and right near him, slithering in among the new eggs, was a snake. Not a big snake, but a snake for sure, flowing as water, silent as night.

Tina yelled; Dad yelled; Mum, who just that moment appeared at the door, yelled; Jonathan quacked; the chickens clucked. The snake must have been terrified by the commotion, for in half a second it had disappeared, as swift and sudden as lightning, through the hole in the corner of the chicken house where it must have got in. And it was never seen again.

Dad turned to Mum. 'Well –' he began.

'I must say – ' Mum interrupted.

Tina finished for them, '– isn't he the cleverest duck in the world?'

Mum and Dad looked at each other. They raised their eyebrows.

'He's got a good alarm system,' Dad said.

'Not bad at all,' Mum agreed. They hugged Tina, and watched Jonathan waddling happily in among the compost in the corner of the chicken pen, getting his lovely feathers all dirty.

Quack . . . quack . . . quack . . . QUACK! he said loudly, and went off to tell Jemima.

SOPHIE MASSON was born in Indonesia of French parents and brought up mainly in Australia. She is the prolific published author of 30 novels in Australia for adults, young adults and children. Sophie has also had novels published in the United States, England and Germany, and numerous short stories in anthologies, magazines and newspapers around the world. Her interest in Arthurian legend is of very long standing and she is the current President of the Arthurian Association of Australia. Sophie lives in Armidale, New South Wales, with her husband and three children. Visit Sophie's website at www.northnet.com.au/~smasson

Pinquo Goes Berserk

EXCERPT FROM *PINQUO*
COLIN THIELE

PINQUO had gone berserk. Whether or not he had just come home from a day's fishing they couldn't tell, but he was carrying on as he had never done before. First he rushed down the side of Dr Piper's house into the backyard. A few moments later he came hurtling back, shepherding Pinquette and Fisho in front of him, together with a couple of other penguin pairs that had recently adopted the place as their home.

He was like a creature possessed. Throughout the panic, as he was herding his family together, he seemed to be issuing orders and sending messages – yapping, crying, gurgling in a frenzy as if his life depended on it. When he had rounded up his relatives he left them standing momentarily near the front gate and rushed off across the sandy sedge-patch towards the beach, yapping and babbling like a maniac. Droves of other penguins were answering him on all sides. Their cries seemed to be just as urgent, just as passionate. Dozens were streaming up out of the sea now, even though it was much too early for their normal home-coming. They came scuttling up the sand in such desperate haste that they were colliding, falling on their faces, leaping up and rushing forwards again as if pursued by all the demons in the world.

Pinquo leapt and dashed about among them like a dervish, yapping and yabbering in a greater frenzy than ever. All round him a pandemonium of answering cries rose up until the air was filled with such a din that Kirsty held her hands to her ears. Suddenly he dashed up to the spot where she and Dr Piper were standing. He came at such a pace that he cannoned into her shin. She leapt back with a yell, but before she had recovered her balance he had rushed round her two or three times like a dwarf weaving a spell, stopped momentarily in front of Dr Piper with a gabble of yaps as if passing on a message of the most desperate and overwhelming importance, and then raced off again. But this time, instead of bursting his way back through the others towards the sea, he gathered up his family and shot off towards the jetty.

The others followed. In pairs and groups, in lines and streams, past rocks and sedges they came hurrying headlong until they emerged onto the open roadway past Dr Piper's white picket fence and Mrs Hempel's sagging gate. They were like an army of little soldiers racing to charge the enemy. In an instant Kirsty and Dr Piper were engulfed by them. Their shoes and shins were buffeted by a steel-blue sea, a rippling wave of heads and backs and flippers that surged on irresistibly, sweeping past them like a flood flinging itself round posts or pylons.

'Good Lord,' said Dr Piper again, holding onto his glasses for fear that they were going to be jolted from his nose and trampled underfoot.

Kirsty was beside herself. 'What's happening?' she cried. 'What on earth is going on?'

'There must be a thousand of them,' said Dr Piper in a daze. 'The whole colony. Every last one.'

'Look,' shouted Kirsty. 'They're heading for the town.' She yelled her disbelief. '*They're going up the main street!*'

Now other noises and cries came back to them above the sounds of the stampeding penguins. The townspeople were caught up in the ruckus just as Kirsty and Dr Piper had been. There were yells of 'Look out!' and 'What's up?'. Shrieks, exclamations, and anxious shouts echoed everywhere.

'There must be a reason,' said Dr Piper, looking over the top of his glasses in amazement. 'It's not normal behaviour.'

In spite of all the drama around them, Kirsty laughed. 'No,' she said, 'it's not.'

'It's too early in the day for them to come ashore,' he said. 'And they never dash off inland like that.'

'But where are they going?' asked Kirsty. 'For heaven's sake.'

The penguins were nearing the far end of the main street – a rippling mass that looked for all the world like a flock of little sheep. They were still being led by a single penguin – a small figure at the head of a family cluster that was in the van of the main army. Pinquo.

At the end of the street they veered left and pressed up the slope towards the higher ground.

'Baker's Knob,' cried Kirsty. 'They're heading for Baker's Knob.'

'For the high ground,' he said.

They both paused and looked at one another with wide eyes.

'The legend,' Kirsty cried breathlessly. 'The legend of the Aboriginal people. The story of the fleeing penguins.'

He spun round. 'It's a warning. A warning of great danger.'

Then he seized her arm and ran forward. 'Quick,' he cried. She hesitated uncertainly but he pulled her so hard that he almost lifted her from the ground. 'Run,' he shouted. 'Run for your life.'

For an old man he moved with astonishing speed. 'Why didn't I think of it before?' he kept saying. 'Why didn't I *think*?'

They raced past the jetty and came pounding up towards the hotel. He was straining hard and wheezing, constantly looking back over his right shoulder towards the sea. He burst in through the hotel door, panting desperately and shouted at the top of his voice. 'Run! Run for your lives!'

Charlie Hilbig's head popped out round the dining-room door. 'What's that?' he asked in alarm.

'Get out, get out,' yelled Dr Piper. 'Get everybody out. You've only got a few minutes. Maybe only a few seconds.'

Charlie's head jolted in fright. 'Where to?'

'The high ground. Baker's Knob. Follow the penguins.'

Dr Piper raced out with Kirsty. 'Run ahead,' he cried. 'Warn everyone. Tell them to hurry, hurry, hurry! There's a tidal wave coming!'

COLIN THIELE was born on 16 November 1920 at Eudunda, in South Australia. He grew up on a farm, and during his childhood there were not many books available. When he was eleven he began his writing career with a long novel about pirates and buried treasure, which he later burned. He has published over 100 books, including the multi award-winning *Storm Boy* (1963), *Blue Fin* (1969) and *The Fire in the Stone* (1973). Colin has received many Australian and international awards, including the Netherlands Award of the Silver Pencil, the Miles Franklin Award, the Dromkeen Medal, Mystery Writers of Americas Inc, the Austrian State Prize for Children's Books (twice), and numerous Children's Book Council of Australia Awards.

The Dare

SIMON HIGGINS

TODD trudged for the ruins on the hill as the full moon climbed behind him inside a milky halo. Somewhere far beyond the crumbling walls ahead a farm dog howled. Todd stopped, counting. Its baleful cries cut the still, cool night for almost thirty seconds. Then the foreboding silence returned. He blinked up at the eerie landscape of jagged shadows round a moonlit, roofless shell, now only a hundred metres away. Turning, Todd snuck a wistful look at the sleeping town way down the slope behind him. That afternoon's big moment came back vividly.

On the footy field, Andrew, all spiky red hair, long arms and sinews, had breathed onion sandwich breath on him again, while reminding him that he was an outsider, not born or raised in Humpybodong, not really welcome in their school. Though not so politely!

'But,' he'd protested, 'before the bank transferred Dad here, we did live in the tablelands, at Gunyastrife. That should count!'

Tall Andrew had frowned, then glanced at Turtle, his gang's plump, bespectacled adviser.

'Nah,' the boy had snorted. 'Gunyastrifers are girls. You want in, it's The Test.'

With that, Big Barry had given a menacing nod, ending any debate.

The Humpy Crew had then detailed the rules. Steal a whiteboard marker. Go to the convict ruins, above town, by the track beside the rusty water tanks. Graffiti the innermost wall – *by moonlight*.

'Remember what happened up there?' Turtle's beady eyes had twinkled.

Andrew had told it with relish. The last convict to work there, a big man loaned to the settlers as a labourer, had turned bushranger. But first, he'd killed the whole family in their farm house. Their dogs too and even, Turtle had added quickly, their defenceless chooks.

'He used his chains on them.' Andrew had licked his lips while saying it. 'One full moon. Like tonight.'

Big Barry had eye-balled him coldly, cracking his knuckles. 'Toddy won't go in, he's a Gunya girlie.'

Calling him *Toddy* had actually helped him to say, 'Yeah? Just watch me!'

'We will,' Andrew had folded his arms. 'But you won't know from where.'

Now, drawing close to the ruins, Todd wasn't feeling so angry, or so brave. He wondered where they'd be hiding, if the plan was to spring out and spook him, or maybe even bash him.

He stared at the entrance to The Test. A half-collapsed rock wall before the old stone homestead looked like a row of teeth, silver and white under the moon's glow. The broken walls of the derelict building rose behind it like giant head-stones. From the rubble and dark shadows came the rank smell of a dead animal. Todd swallowed hard, but went in anyway.

Only metres from the innermost wall, as he fumbled for the marker in his pocket – which he preferred to think of as *borrowed* – Todd heard a sound. The wind, he told himself quickly, ignoring the fact that there *was* no wind. He tried not to, but gave in to considering the sound's character. Metal, clinking, like his weekend bike repairs. Or chains, dragging over masonry. His blood turned to ice.

Another *clink*. Todd crouched low, his thoughts racing. Denial was pointless. He'd heard it twice now and it *had to be* the ghost of –

Wait. He winced, cursing quietly. This was a set-up! One of them had hidden inside this ruin, near the target wall, to flick a bike chain or something on a rock and freak him out. A routine they'd probably used on a dozen victims.

Todd brushed the earth round him until he found a dry branch to serve as a club. Then, shuffling forward, low to the ground, he slowly closed on the inner wall. Anxious and angry all at once, he carefully circled its decaying pale surfaces, his feet avoiding the twigs and soft drink cans that the moonlight revealed. Nothing! He straightened up with a sigh. Todd dropped the club, pulling the marker from his pocket.

A few seconds after he'd inscribed his name, with an excla-mation mark to emphasise how boldly he'd defied their test, the sound came again, this time from behind the wall itself. Behind it, or *inside* it? Todd gaped, his eyes stretching wide. Then he heard the metallic rattle, louder, and longer than ever. Clearly, *on the move*.

That did it. Twisting back for the entrance, Todd broke into a sprint, but started stumbling over rubble and cans, snapping twigs, catching his toes in brush. His mouth turned dry. He knew that whoever – whatever – was in here, *it* knew exactly where he was!

He kicked a bottle and sent it smashing, tumbled over an old cardboard carton then, yelping from fresh bruises, sprang to his feet and charged for a gap in the wall yawning in front of him. But as he reached it, a tall, solid silhouette blocked his path, and Todd caught the glint of metal in the moonlight, against one of the figure's legs. The ghost strode forward. With a strangled cry, Todd collapsed to his belly, clawing in the rising, moonbeam-lit dust for a new weapon.

'Easy, boy!' A very human voice suddenly chuckled above him, followed by the metal sound again. 'Just keep your hands outa ya mouth.' Todd raised his head slowly, squinting up at the silhouette. A *friendly* killer ghost?

Twenty minutes later, Todd sat at a wooden table in a farm-house hidden by trees along the track he'd climbed, a mug of chocolate steaming between his palms. The farmer's wife smiled knowingly as he explained the dare.

The tall old man swung his creaking leg to rest beside Todd's chair. 'Me great-grandpa owned this selection, only *he* didn't have to work it wearing a caliper. Polio.' He winked. 'That convict yarn's all bollocks. And you're not the first kid I've had to shoo outa there before he touched a poison fox-bait in the dark.'

Todd nodded slowly, embarrassed.

'Well, anyhow,' the farmer grinned, 'about that mob's stupid test thing: I reckon ya passed.'

SIMON HIGGINS is an author whose employment history reads like a novel. He's been a police officer, a disc jockey, prosecutor, licensed private investigator, and a monster in a sideshow Ghost Train, which he regards as the pinnacle of his working life. Now a full-time novelist, Simon's bent for adventure includes such hobbies as shipwreck diving and martial arts, a passion that took him to Japan and China. Simon's books reflect his interests. His dark crime thrillers *Doctor Id, Cybercage* and *The Stalking Zone* have all been published internationally. *Thunderfish*, the first of Simon's futuristic sea adventure series, made the best-seller lists. Its sequel, *Under No Flag*, was short-listed for a Ned Kelly Award. Visit Simon's website at www.homepages.better.net.au/doctorid

Fair Ground

EXCERPT FROM *YOU'RE DROPPED*
ANDREW DADDO

WE ALWAYS looked forward to the Show, even though Clint pretended that he didn't. He was doing a lot of pretending lately about not liking the things he liked. That was the price of cool. Soon he wasn't going to need to pretend because he really *wouldn't* like it. Lizzie was there now. She'd been over the Show for ages.

For the first time, Mum and Dad weren't coming. There was usually one of them hanging around to make sure we didn't get into too much trouble, but this time, instead of coming, they gave us a lecture. It was so long and stupid, I wished they had been coming so that we wouldn't have had to listen to it. Dad talked about the dangers that lurked everywhere and how you had to watch the watchers. He nodded a lot and we nodded back. There were promises and back-up promises and vows of goodness that none of us really intended to keep. We just had to make Mum and Dad feel better about letting us go by ourselves. At the last minute Mum said she would come – just in case. But Dad said there was a time when boys needed to be boys and stand on their own four feet.

'That's two each,' he laughed. He dropped us at the community centre and pressed a twenty into each of our hands.

'Is that it?' asked Clint.

'Afraid so. You should count yourself lucky,' Dad said. 'Back in my day, when the Show came to town I'd be lucky to get twenty *cents*, let alone –' Clint closed the car door on the story we heard every time the Show came round. 'Your brother's in charge!' Dad yelled through the closed window, but it was hard to know which brother he meant. Clint and I looked at each other and smiled. Cool! No one was in charge.

The Show looked good. It always did at night. They parked the trucks and caravans out of sight and the lights from the rides and sideshow alley made it look exciting instead of skuzzy – which was how it looked in daylight. I wondered how Lizzie could ever have stopped liking it. She was always changing, but the time she *really* turned weird was after she got her first bra.

She and Mum had planned it in a morning of giggles and whispers at the kitchen table. Dad had a strango attack. He kept asking if she really needed a bra anyway and I have to admit the thought had crossed my mind as well. She was sitting at the table in a tight Madonna T-shirt and she said her breasts looked like the noses on a pair of puppy dogs straining at the leash.

'She's just a kid,' Dad said to no one in particular.

'It's not *really* as if you'd understand, Ridley,' Mum said to him. He looked as if he was about to argue, but had thought better of it. Mum and Lizzie went back to their giggling and whispering.

When Lizzie went to her room to get ready Mum said to

Dad, 'Just make it special, okay. It's a big day for her, so please, don't stuff it up.'

'Yeah, yeah, okay. I won't,' he said. He looked as if he meant it, too. 'I'll make sure it's a day she never forgets.'

'Good,' said Mum.

'Good,' nodded Dad.

'Good,' they said together. She kissed him and left with Lizzie.

'Stuff it up? She's kidding, isn't she? Why would I do that?' He was muttering to himself as he fossicked around in the pantry. 'We should celebrate, don't you reckon?' I shrugged, I didn't know what the big deal was. It was only a bra. Mum wore one all the time and nobody said anything about that. 'Let's make a cake.' He smiled and I felt my mouth go a bit moist at the thought of licking the bowl.

Dad found a cake mix and grabbed the cake tins out of the cupboard. 'What do you reckon? This one?' It was the shape of a love heart. Mum used it every Valentine's Day to make a cake for Dad. I nodded.

Making the cake was too easy. Even I could have done it, but Dad carried on as if it was a real achievement. We licked the bowl while it cooked.

Then he called Gon and Pop.

The cake was good, but it was the icing that was the real winner. Dad wrote 'Congratulations' down the bottom, near the point of the heart in big red letters. 'That ought to do it.' He smiled.

'It needs more,' I said, but I didn't know what.

'How about –' But instead of finishing the sentence, he took a tube of icing and started to draw. In the middle of each mound up at the top of the heart, he drew a large triangle. And by the time he'd finished the second one, I could see exactly what he was doing. It was awesome. He'd drawn a bra. Cool. I had no idea he could ice like that. He put two candles on the cake: right in the middle of each bra cup.

'Bit dodgy!' He laughed. 'Now listen, Fergus, if your mum reckons this bra thing is a big deal for Lizzie, then it's a big deal, okay? If you're going to stir her, you can go somewhere else. No teasing.' And he said it with a twinkle in his eye that made me wonder.

When Mum and Lizzie came home, they were still giggling. Each of them had an armload of shopping bags and once again I noticed that the only bags Mum ever whinged about carrying were the grocery kind. Lizzie had a huge one from Bras and Things.

'Crikey, darl!' squawked Dad when they came into the kitchen. He'd just covered his cake with a tea towel. 'How many'd you get? She'll grow out of them in five minutes, won't she?'

Mum gave him The Look, but softened. 'There's a surprise in there for you too, Riddles.'

'Hey? From Bras and Things? What could I possibly want from there?'

She winked at him and this ridiculous smile crept across his face.

'Oh, YUK!' Lizzie and I said. It was the first time we'd agreed on anything for ages.

'How'd you go then, princess?' Dad asked. But it was pretty obvious. Her T-shirt was hanging off her shoulder and you could see her bra strap. It was red.

'Daaaaaaaaaad!'

He gave her a kiss and she smiled through her embarrass-ment. Mum was beaming: Dad had done well.

There was a knock at the back door and Gon and Pop

followed it. When Lizzie turned to say hello to them, Dad flicked her bra strap.

'Get out,' she said playfully.

'Mmm hmm. You'll have to watch that, now.'

'Daaaaaaaaaad!' Lizzie smiled for the second time that morning.

'So, what's the celebration? Why did we have to rush over here?' asked Pop. He sounded a bit annoyed. Everyone knew Saturday morning was Pop's time to pick winners – and not the ones up his nose. Gon didn't look too fussed. She was glad of any excuse for a visit – if she bothered with one at all. Mum looked at Dad with the kind of look a cat gives a ball of string.

'You ready, Fergus?' he asked. I nodded and pulled down the blind while he bent over to the bench in the corner, lighting the candles on the cake.

Everyone was smiling. Dad straightened up. 'One, two, sing!' he said, so I did.

'Happy bra day to you,

Happy bra day to you,

Happy bra day, dear Lizzie,

Happy bra day to yooooou!'

Dad put the cake on the table. Mum looked as if she was going to have a heart attack. I think Gon *did*. Pop started laughing and Lizzie looked as if she was melting. She crossed her arms over her new bra and ran out of the room, silently screaming.

Mum ran after Lizzie and Gon ran after Mum.

Dad's jaw dropped. He looked around for help but there was none in the kitchen that morning.

ANDREW DADDO began his work in television at Network Ten. He then spent time at the Nine Network as Professor Plum, before moving to the Seven Network, where he hosted *Australia's Funniest People*, *World's Greatest Commercials* and *TV WEEK Logie Awards*. In 1999, Andrew co-hosted *Kidspeak* with Ernie Dingo. In 2002 he teamed up once again with Ernie Dingo as a presenter on *The Great Outdoors* and hosted *World's Greatest Commercials* and the *Ozspell Australian Spelling Championships*. Andrew also writes for children. *Sprung!*, *Writing in Wet Cement* and *You're Dropped!* are some of his titles. He likes fishing, golf, travelling and spending time with his family.

Index of Authors

Acknowledgements

1. • 'Licked' from *Unbearable!* by Paul Jennings
First published by Penguin Books Australia Ltd,
1999
Copyright © Paul Jennings, 1999

2. • 'My Enemy' from *Party Animals* by Christine
Harris
Previously published as Widdershins by Random
House Australia, 1995
Copyright © Christine Harris, 1995

3. • 'Brolga and Jabiru' from *Aboriginal Myths
and Legends: Age-old Stories of Australian Tribes*
selected by Roland Robinson
The Hamlyn Publishing Group Limited, 1969.
Copyright © Roland Robinson, 1969

4. • 'Dot Meets a Deadly Snake' an extract from
Dot and the Kangaroo by Ethel Pedley
Angus & Robertson Australia,1899.
Copyright © Ethel Pedley, 1899.

5. • 'Bett-Bett' an extract from *The Little Black
Princess* by Mrs Aeneas Gunn
First published by Angus & Robertson,1905.
Angus & Robertson's *More Australian Children's
Classics* edition.
Copyright © Aeneas Gunn, 1905.

6. • 'I Want to See a Human' an extract from
Snugglepot and Cuddlepie
First published in Australia by Angus & Robertson
(an imprint of HarperCollins),1940.
Bluegum edition first published, 1984.
The story by May Gibbs was published with the
kind permission of The Northcott Society and The
Spastic Centre of New South Wales.
Copyright © The Spastic Centre of NSW and The
Northcott Society, 1940

7. • 'Sing to Me' (a traditional story) from *Tell Me
Another Tale* edited by Jean Chapman
First published by Hodder & Stroughton, 1974.
Text copyright © Jean Chapman, 1974

8. • 'The Flood-Maker' (a traditional story) from *Tell
Me Another Tale* edited by Jean Chapman
First published by Hodder & Stroughton, 1974.
Text copyright © Jean Chapman, 1974

9. • 'Introducing the Bomb' an extract from *Don't
Pat the Wombat!* by Elizabeth Honey
First published by Allen & Unwin,1996,
Paperback edition, 2000.
Text copyright © Elizabeth Honey, 1996

10. • *The Bugalugs Bum Thief* by Tim Winton
First published by Penguin Books Australia Ltd,
1998
Text copyright © Tim Winton, 1998

11. • 'I Wasn't Good at Anything: a stand-up
comedy routine by Gary Gaggs' from *Selby's
Selection* by Duncan Ball
First published by Harper Collins, 2001.
Text copyright © Duncan Ball, 2001

12. • 'Bertie the Bear' by Pixie O'Harris
First published in the Pixie O'Harris Story Book,
1940.
Copyright © Pixie O'Harris, 1940.

13. • 'Bunyip Blue Gum Leaves Home' an extract
from *The Magic Pudding* by Norman Lindsay
First published in Australia by Angus & Robertson
(an imprint of HarperCollins), 1918.
New Bluegum Australian Children's Classic
edition, 2000.
Copyright © Janet Glad, 1918

14. • *The Wish* by Deborah Abela
Reproduced by kind permission of Deborah Abela.
Copyright © Deborah Abela, 2003

15. • *Haunted* by Victor Kelleher
Reproduced by permission of Victor Kelleher, care
of Margaret Connolly & Associates Pty Ltd
Copyright © Victor Kelleher, 2003

Acknowledgements

16. • 'Born in the Wild Wind' an extract from *The Silver Brumby* by Elyne Mitchell
By arrangement with the copyright holder, Elyne Mitchell Estate of Curtis Brown (Aust) Pty Ltd
First published by Hutchinson & Co. Ltd in 1958
Copyright © Elyne Mitchell, 1958

17. • 'Blinky Finds a New Home' an extract from *Blinky Bill* by Dorothy Wall
First published in Australia by Angus & Robinson (an imprint of HarperCollins), 1939.
Bluegum edition first published, 1985.
Copyright © HarperCollins Publishers Pty Ltd, 1939, 1985

18. • *Gran's Beaut Ute* by Margaret Clark
Reproduced with kind permission of Margaret Clark.
Copyright © Margaret Clark, 2003

19. • 'Ms White's Garden' by Vashti Farrer
First published in *School Magazine*, 'Countdown' (Vol 85 No 2), March 2000.
Text copyright © Vashti Farrer, 2000

20. • 'Introducing the Very Naughty Mother' an extract from *The Very Naughty Mother Goes Green* by Gretel Killeen, first published by Random House Australia, 2002. This is the first book in a series that includes *The Very Naughty Mother Goes Invisible*, *The Very Naughty Mother Runs Away* and *The Very Naughty Mother is a Spy*.
Copyright © Gretel Killeen, 2002

21. • *Slam Jam Sam* by Mike Dumbleton
Written by Mike Dumbleton, 1999
Copyright © Mike Dumbleton, 2003

22. • 'The Hippolottamuss' by Nan Hunt first published in *Can I Keep Him?*: Stories about Pets
Oxford University Press, 1991.
Copyright © Nan Hunt, 1991

23. • 'Friday' and 'Saturday' an extract from *Penny Pollard's Diary* by Robin Klein
First published by Oxford University Press, 1983.
This extract reproduced with the permission of the publisher, Hodder Headline Australia.
Text copyright © Robin Klein, 1983

24. • *Moving on* by Maggie Hamilton
Reproduced with kind permission of Maggie Hamilton.
Copyright © Maggie Hamilton, 2003

25. • 'The Hairyman' an extract from *My Girragundji* by Meme McDonald and Boori Monty Pryor
Allen & Unwin, 1998.
Text copyright © Meme McDonald and Boori Monty Pryor, 1998

26. • 'The Birthday Surprise' an extract from *The Adventures of the Muddle-headed Wombat* (The Muddle-headed Wombat on Holiday) by Ruth Park.
The Muddle-headed Wombat on Holiday first published, 1964.
Combined edition first published by Angus & Robertson (an imprint of HarperCollins), 1979.
Classics edition, 1990.
By arrangement with the copyright holder, Ruth Park of Curtis Brown (Aust) Pty Ltd
Copyright © Kemalde Pty Ltd, 1964 and 1979

27. • 'Duck's Luck' by Sophie Masson
First published in *School Magazine*, 'Countdown' (Vol 86 No 3), April 2001.
Reproduced by permission of Sophie Masson, care of Margaret Connolly & Associates.
Text copyright © Sophie Masson, 2001

28. • 'Pinquo Goes Berserk' an extract from *Pinquo* by Colin Thiele
First published by Rigby Publishers, 1983.
Reprinted by Lansdowne Publishing Pty Ltd, 1996.
Reproduced with permission of the publisher, New Holland Publishers.
Copyright © Colin Thiele, 1983

29. • The Dare by Simon Higgins
Written by Simon Higgins, 1990
Copyright © Simon Higgins, 2003

30. • Extract from 'Fair Ground' in You're Dropped by Andrew Daddo (illustrations by Terry Denton)
First published by Mark Macleod Books, Hodder Headline Australia, 2003.
Text copyright © Andrew Daddo, 2003

Linsay Knight

Linsay Knight is widely respected as a leading expert in and contributor to Australian children's literature. As the Managing Editor and Children's Book Publisher at Random House Australia for ten years, Linsay nurtured the talent of numerous authors and illustrators to create some of Australia's most successful children's books.

Linsay is also the author of several successful children's books in *The Macquarie Beginner Book* series and is the co-author of titles such as *The Macquarie Young Kids' Dictionary* and *The Dictionary of Performing Arts in Australia* Volumes 1 and 2.

She currently lives in London with her husband.

Gregory Rogers

Gregory Rogers studied fine art at the Queensland College of Art and has illustrated a large number of educational and trade children's picture books.

In 1995, Gregory won the Kate Greenaway Medal for his illustrations in *Way Home*. *Way Home* also won a parents' Choice Award in the US and was shortlisted for the ABPA book design awards.

Gregory's most recent picture books include *Beyond the Dusk* by Victor Kelleher, *The Gift* by Libby Hathorn and *Princess Max* by Laurie Stiller for Random House Australia.